Praise

'Building a legacy is about
than we found it! *Gaming For Good* explains how
gaming can shape human behaviour to transform
the world's biggest challenges into even greater
opportunities – from achieving carbon neutrality to
how we use the planet's finite resources, the answer
might be in the games we love to play.'
— **Bill McDermott**, Chief Executive Officer
(CEO) and Chairman, ServiceNow

'*Gaming For Good* is a brilliant book about how
the world of games can save the world! We're
now halfway through the most important goals
of our time, the United Nations' (UN) Sustainable
Development Goals (SDGs), and we really can use
cultural mega-trends such as Games to take action
today. This book shows how. Read – play – change
the world!'
— **Richard Curtis**, Writer, Director and
Co-Founder of Comic Relief

'The games industry has huge potential to drive
massive awareness and action to protect our planet.
We are running out of time and global megatrends
such as gaming are a great way to inspire generations
of all ages. In *Gaming For Good*, Jude and Mathias
use their years of expertise to demystify the industry
today and make it practical for all, from working
within it to the industry taking action. Whether

you know a lot about games or not, this book is a must read if you want to do something big to save our planet.'

— **Boaz Paldi**, Chief Creative Officer (CCO), UNDP

'Our planet is facing challenges that our generation has to solve. The Intergovernmental Panel on Climate Change (IPCC) is very clear, and with unambitious targets that are not even met, we have to think outside the box. Jude and Mathias do that in *Gaming For Good*. With facts, passion and examples, they make the case for games perhaps being the media platform that can inspire and enable change. With their massive audiences and attention, game makers are strategically positioned to change the world. They must use their powers wisely, and this book points them in the right direction.'

— **José María Figueres**, ex-President of Costa Rica and former CEO of World Economic Forum

'With a potential audience of 5 billion players by 2030, games are poised to become one of the most impactful forms of entertainment and a powerful vehicle to raise awareness of global issues, like the fight against climate change. I believe games have a unique ability to educate, empower and engage players by immersing them in beautiful virtual environments and showing them how their actions

can have a direct impact on the world around them. It is essential we as an industry play our part to continue reducing our environmental footprint while also encouraging our communities to act and lead the change.'
— **Yves Guillemot**, Co-founder and CEO, Ubisoft

'In this crucial period of the twenty-first century, the world must unite and turn intention into action to avert climate and nature crises. Gaming has incredible global reach and the potential to inspire change.'
— **Professor Kieren Mayers**, Senior Director of Environment, Social and Governance, Sony Interactive Entertainment

'As someone who is passionate about using games for social impact, I found *Gaming For Good* to be a valuable resource. Jude Ower and Mathias Nørvig's conversations with industry leaders about how the industry is tackling real-world issues are both thought-provoking and inspiring. *Gaming For Good* is a fascinating read that showcases how the games industry can be a force for good. Through interviews with leaders of successful studios, the book highlights practical strategies for making sustainable development a core part of the games industry.'
— **Nic Walker**, Chief Operating Officer (COO), Space Ape Games

'*Gaming For Good* offers a comprehensive examination of the current landscape and major players in impact games, and an exciting look at what the future holds – not only for the gaming industry, but for the large cross-sector community united by a vision to use games and play to make the world a better place.'
— **Susanna Pollack**, CEO, Games for Change

'It is encouraging that this book is talking about the opportunity and responsibility the gaming industry has to use its reach to influence positive change in the climate debate. Our lovely planet needs every industry to take responsibility.'
— **René Rechtman**, CEO and Founder, Moonbug Entertainment

'The planet needs concrete action. Games and digital experiences – low-carbon entertainment – are the approach to degrowth that has the best chances of working. The games industry's incredible talent, passion and experience in building compelling products is such a special capability of our civilisation. Jude and Mathias's book positions it to help solve global issues instead of simply producing "fun".'
— **David Helgason**, Founder, Unity Technologies

GAMING FOR GOOD

Unlock the power of gaming to
create a better world for us all

Jude Ower and Mathias Gredal Nørvig

Rethink

First published in Great Britain in 2024
by Rethink Press (www.rethinkpress.com)

To our families who have been our rocks and have believed in us throughout this crazy journey.

To my lovely doughnuts Chris (Tiff), Cornelius and Hamish, I love you to the moon and back!
– Jude

To the cool kids Leo, Johan, Julius, Amalie and my beloved Charlotte. Never a dull moment with you guys.

– Mathias

Contents

Foreword

'Will you write a foreword?', they asked. Sure, I thought. That would be a privilege. As long as the UN don't mind (which they didn't). But what to write?

You shouldn't wish for a book to 'date'. Ideally, it should stand the test of time, well-thumbed and spine-cracked through heavy use. But I do hope this book ages, and quickly.

That's not to say anything negative about it – it's written by two fine minds – who've both been critical to the success of the Playing for the Planet initiative – with great insights from those at the centre of this industry. But it's important to view it as a snapshot of where we stand today – the first chapter, if you like – as there is still so much more to come.

The book takes a broad view on the contributions the industry can make to influencing change. When it comes to global carbon emissions, the gaming industry does not compare to other energy intensive sectors, such as construction or transport.

But as games get richer, faster and more immersive, energy demands will grow. Acting on this will not to be without its challenges, but sections of the industry are starting to put their best foot forward on this. It's through collaboration that change is starting to happen. However, this group of leaders needs to grow with urgency; the premium we need to work with, not perfection.

The true superpower of this sector is the stories they tell. Games are fun, offering a thrilling escape into other worlds. Authentically harnessing play-with-purpose is where it gets interesting. Research shows that most gamers do deeply care about the environment. We've been exploring this with studios over the past four years through the Green Game Jam, building an assumption-free evidence base is the next step.

I remain more convinced than ever that the video games industry can make a significant offer on addressing the triple planetary crises of climate, nature and pollution. While other books will follow, the pages of this one are a solid record of the current state of play and the case for gaming's role in addressing environmental issues.

Enjoy the pages that follow. We look forward to seeing what comes next.

Sam Barratt, Chief, Youth, Education and Advocacy of the UN Environment Programme

Introduction

Passion. Grit. Serendipity. Urgency.

You are a global leader. Your mission is to stop the world temperature from rising another 1.5 degrees Celsius. You have the power to make changes in six different categories: land and oceans, infrastructure and cities, farms and food, energy, protecting people and green economy. How will you do it?

This was the mission that gamers worldwide were tasked with during 2020 through in-game ads and invitations to play. The game, called *Mission 1.5*, was a chance to learn about the climate while playing with options to reduce or increase the temperature of the planet, the ultimate goal being to stop global warming by another 1.5 degrees Celsius. In reality, we must do this. So far, we are not on track to achieve it…

The results from the survey conducted by *Mission 1.5*, the biggest ever of its kind, representing 56% of the global population, became known as 'The Peoples' Climate Vote'.[1] It showed world leaders that, in every single country, the majority of citizens believe that climate change is not only real, but something that demands urgent action.

Within mobile games, a sample size of more than 1.2 million people worldwide, representing all demographics, were consulted as to their views on climate action, including those that were most affected by it. Through the UN Development Programme (UNDP), the results were presented to world leaders in 2021, stressing their agency to change climate policies fast.

The survey was the first of its kind due to the sheer volume of responses and speed at which the data was collected. It was the first of its kind because the only way to gather such information from global citizens with such speed and scale was through mobile gaming.

Why? Because gaming reaches a huge volume of global citizens and can engage them in the topic of climate policy quickly and efficiently. No other method could distil the complex message of the National Determined Contributions (NDCs) – the contributions countries make as stated in the Paris Climate Change Agreement – in a way that would engage so many people. Subsequently, the data from the survey was used at the G20 in 2021 and included in the report from the Intergovernmental Panel on Climate Change, the IPCC, in 2022.[2]

Games were instrumental in gathering the voices of people globally and amassing data at speed and scale. *Mission 1.5* is one striking example of how the billions of gamers worldwide and the games industry can be a force for progress. This is true not only when it comes to global warming; the industry can also be used to address other urgent issues such as poverty, social justice, diversity and education. Everywhere, from Kenya to the United States, games and gamers are helping to solve complex problems, creating awareness of the need for change and showing viable alternatives.

This book is the first of its kind. It is intended to get us to look at the world around us, and the virtual world, a little differently. How can the virtual world help us live on a healthier and more sustainable planet? It shines a light on how truly ubiquitous games have become. Not only does the games industry today far outsize other entertainment categories such as movies and books, it is unique in the way that games allow the gamers to have a say; it is not just one-way communication. Gamers can interact and respond and suggest, which means that games can be leveraged to be a powerful force for change.

The book will show how the games industry can help mobilise other sectors to up their game, and why collaboration is key. We highlight examples of this which, until recently, have mainly only been known inside the industry itself. We will show how movements are bringing like-minded companies together across sectors to amplify the impact they generate, and to support and motivate each other's efforts.

This book is about unlocking the huge potential of one of the fastest-growing industries. It shows how a combined brain trust of the games industry's leaders is trying to grapple with the power of using games for good, across sectors and challenges, to help drive a healthier and more sustainable planet, turning our online actions into real-world impact.

It tells the story of how showing 43 billion visual cues to 150 million players in *Subway Surfers* has helped drive awareness and inspire action. How games are raising hundreds of millions of dollars through selling in-game items such as character skins. How initiatives like *Mission 1.5* and 'The Peoples' Climate Vote' can be among the most important ways to engage the global population in planetary matters, getting into the minds of politicians.

The topic of Games For Good has been covered in amazing books, such as *Reality is Broken* by Jane McGonigal[3] and *Moral Combat* by Patrick Markey and Christopher Ferguson.[4] With tons of interviews, surveys and case studies, we build on this ground-breaking thinking to show how games are being deployed and the opportunity we have today in 2023 and beyond.

This is very much a passion project, for us as authors as well as for the numerous people who have helped make the book a reality, and hopefully for you as our reader. Passion for people and for the planet.

This is what gets us up in the morning and sometimes keeps us up at night.

The evidence is clear. The latest IPCC report is concise and concrete,[5] and we are currently not on the right trajectory as a society. Many factors can help us get there, but we need more passion at all levels. We would love to see international state-level institutions and politicians do more, but we think that there is even more power to be unleashed from private companies and individuals. In this book, we explore this power specifically through games as a platform for change.

This just doesn't happen by itself. It takes grit.

Things really started to take off when Jude hosted one of her Play Nice dinners in 2018, at the Game Developer Conference (GDC) in San Francisco. Through a number of Play Nice dinners in previous years, and her countless meetings on the sustainability agenda, she knew a handful of people who just had to be there. Everyone attending was interested and committed to see how they could engage with games as a force for change. It was here that the industry's largest movement for the planet was born, the Playing for the Planet Alliance, engaging most of the major studios who reach a whopping 1.4 billion monthly active user base.

Three of Jude's new acquaintances were Sam Barratt from the UN Environment Programme (UNEP), Trista Patterson, then at Grid Arendal, now at Microsoft, and Mathias Gredal Nørvig from SYBO, the company behind the world's most downloaded game,

Subway Surfers. They should prove instrumental in formalising the work around the planetary agenda.

Jude remembers:

'At all GDCs [Game Developer Conference] I've been to, there have been plenty of dinners and mixers each night, and when we have hosted Play Nice dinners, we've always got a growing number of attendees join us. But 2018 was different – we had a sense of urgency and people all showed up with ambitions to do something. There was pure alignment around the table. With the UN involved, we changed the conversation from discussions to action, and with Trista dedicating her life to the science on climate change, we had the facts to back it. Mathias became for me the embodiment of personal passion in an executive function, a thought leader from within the industry and a voice of the studios, with the muscle to reach 150 million players.'

Mathias remembers the dinner vividly as well.

'I was off the beaten track at GDC, coming in only knowing a few of the fellow climate-arians, but Jude had really managed to get all the right stakeholders and passionate people around the same table. It all clicked, and I remember leaving the dinner thinking that I'd need to talk more with Jude, Trista and

Sam. As I read through the first Playing for the Planet report, I remember thinking that there is a huge potential to align the games industry, share best practices and push each other to do even more. Jude is the woman that started this whole movement, and I am proud to work with her.'

This is why we two, Jude and Mathias, share a feeling of serendipity. Passion and grit only get you so far. We needed that stroke of luck that brought it all together at the right time. We are thankful that it has played out in an even more collaborative and additive way than we could have ever imagined.

This book is a product of all the hard work done at Jude's company Playmob throughout the years, all the climate actions at SYBO, all the participating companies of the alliance Playing for the Planet and all the fellow thought-leaders from the games industry. All quoted text throughout the book, unless referenced otherwise, is taken from personal interviews and used with permission. While it is written on a premise of playfulness, platform potential and planet needs, it guides the conversation and actions in a very specific direction: the right one. Our credo is 'When given a choice, choose right', so when you have two equally good game features, choose the one that is better for the planet, better for diversity, better for spreading kindness.

The aim of this book is to align the world on what gaming is and what the potentials are. We deliberately haven't gone too deep into particular areas, although the temptation was there, because this book is for anyone interested in gaming, from those in the industry who want to realise the power they have and feel proud of what has been achieved so far, to those who collaborate with the industry and those who play who want to better understand how choices in the games they work with and play can impact our planet.

This book is not a dissertation on the perils of gaming. We are fully cognisant of the dangers of people playing too much, some spending more money than they can afford, young ones playing games meant for an older audience, the toxicity of online gaming communities, the need for stronger enforcement of privacy and data. This needs focus as well and we support people with that as their primary topic, but ours is the sustainability of the planet. While we are aware and passionate about the other topics, this book seeks to explore gaming as a platform for good.

We hope you will find our book insightful, join the cause and drive the industry and world in a better direction. We hope we can inspire you to share best practices and use them more widely, and we hope that this book is the first of many that brings good intentions home where they can flourish.

Enjoy!

PART ONE
THREE BILLION GAMERS

'There are 3 billion people who play video games today, which is nearly half the planet, and it's growing faster than the human population. That's an amazing opportunity for us as an industry.'
— Phil Spencer, CEO, Gaming at Microsoft

Today, gaming is for everyone and most people are gamers, even if they don't realise it. Gamers are everywhere; they are you and me, and almost half of the global population plays. That's an estimated 3 billion gamers on the planet. This doesn't include the millions of people who enjoy just watching others play on services such as Twitch and YouTube, or even at live eSports events.

Despite the size of the gaming market, it still remains relatively misunderstood. As Sir Ian Livingstone,

Co-founder of Games Workshop and Hiro Capital, stated:

> 'On a superficial level, games do not enjoy celebrity in the way music or film or TV does, so the people behind the industry are not known and therefore not understood. The only knowledge a non-game player has on the industry and people who play is from the content that they've heard about via media or perhaps seen.'

The majority of gamers today are playing mobile games. They play for around eight hours per week on average, making a total collectively of 24 billion hours per week of playtime – a figure that has increased seven times in the last decade, as has gaming revenue, year on year growing at over 7%.[6] These numbers mean that gaming is a force to be reckoned with – and it is now seeing an increase in its share of wallet, share of time and share of mind. The industry is becoming more and more influential in our daily lives, where reality and the virtual world will blur as the metaverse becomes mainstream. Having this power and share of mind, the gaming industry has the ability to change the world, and our goal is to make this change a positive one.

When we play, we are immersed and deeply engaged. We can't multitask when playing, making gaming a powerful medium which commands our attention. Something so engaging and powerful must be taken seriously; by the industry, the players and other industries outside of gaming. When something so powerful is unleashed into the world, it is our responsibility as humans to really understand the huge opportunity it presents to us all and use it for good, for making a positive, not negative, impact in the world.

To begin with, we need to better understand gaming today, so in this first part of the book we look at who these 3 billion people are. Where are they? What and how do they play? Crucially, what do they want from their games?

1
We All Play Games

'As people grow up, they don't stop playing games.
The type of games or the media mix may change a
little, but it's still part of their life, which means it's a
powerful media tool that has a significant impact on
society and individuals, whether we like it or not.'
— Marc Merrill, Co-chairman, Co-founder,
    Riot Games

Often, if you ask someone whether they are a
gamer, they will say no, because the image that
pops into their head as soon as you mention the word
'gamer' is of a teenage boy playing war games on his
own in his bedroom. This may be how gaming started
back in the seventies, but today it is an old-school way
of thinking about gaming and gamers.

If you follow up that initial question with, 'Do
you play *Candy Crush* or *Sudoku* or *Words with Friends*

on your phone?', they are likely to say, 'Oh yeah, I play those games.' Although they recognise these as games, somehow they don't consider themselves as gamers, yet where console and computer used to dominate, mobile games are now the biggest category of gaming.

The exponential spread of internet access and mobile devices – particularly smartphones – over the last twenty years has given people all over the world easy and inexpensive access to mobile games, which, incidentally, are now Apple's biggest revenue earner. Matt Fischer, Apple's Vice President of the App Store, recalls:

> 'It was hard to imagine just how large an impact mobile gaming would have when we started the App Store in 2008. Since then, we've seen over 1 billion people download games from the App Store and play them on their iPhones as well as on iPads, Macs and Apple TVs. The App Store has gone from just 500 apps and games at its launch in 2008, to 1.8 million apps and games today.'

Another major reason for the explosion of gaming in many markets is the development of the free-to-play model. The player has the option to make in-app purchases to get items or progress in the game, but it is essentially free to download, try and even play. In the lighter version of free-to-play, the games are truly free, although your play will be interrupted by pop-up ads or videos as a means to 'pay' for the game experience. On the heavier end of the spectrum, there are games where the player can try the first levels or a subset of the game before they have to spend money to progress. Then there is everything in between.

There was a massive spike in gaming during the Covid-19 pandemic of 2020–22, when millions of people were unable to meet and socialise in traditional ways. Gaming was not just a way of passing time, a simple form of entertainment during lockdowns and layoffs; it was also a much-needed break and a way to stay social. It helped people connect with their friends and have a joint purpose. Quiz games in particular spiked during Covid.

The economic downturn caused by the pandemic and other global crises also served to increase the popularity of gaming, though perhaps less dramatically. Whereas, for example, a day out at a theme park for a family of four or five might cost £500 or more, a games console and a couple of online games can be purchased for less than half that amount – and provide greater longevity and sustainability with the entertainment. We are, of course, not advocating that we all play games to replace days out, but as a way to have fun and enjoy activities with family and friends which do not cost a lot and can be done more frequently.

As we will see, these factors have impacted the types of people playing games and the nature of gaming itself.

Gamers are everywhere

'Games have enormous power beyond entertainment. For more than two decades, innovators have been using games to drive real-world change, yet we've still only scratched the surface when it comes to the potential of games, and gamers, for social impact. The reach, scale and diversity of the audience give us an enormous opportunity to really activate real-world change.'
— Susanna Pollack, CEO, Games for Change

The stereotypical teenage male gamer is no longer typical. The average age of a gamer or game player today is thirty-seven.[7] The smallest portion of gamers (just 16% or so) are under eighteen, while 20% of them are over fifty. A 2022 survey found that 36% of video game players are in the eighteen to thirty-four age range, and 6% are sixty-five years and older. Ofcom found 62% of UK adults played some form of video game in 2020,[8] and research from GlobalWebIndex found the fifty-six to sixty-four age group was the fastest-growing market, rising by almost a third (32%) since 2018.[9]

Gaming has also traditionally been seen as male dominated in terms of players, but the reality now is that gaming is 50/50 male/female, although of course there are variations in player profiles depending on the game and the platform, as well as the age group. Games like *Football Manager* and *Golf Clash* naturally attract more men, although some women play these types of games. Conversely, games like *Candy Crush* or family-oriented games such as *June's Journey* or *The Sims* tend to be played more by females than males; the split is around 60/40. These are all averages and can vary.

Unfortunately, though, only 22% of those who work in the industry are women,[10] which must change so we have women creating games for women. Initiatives such as Women in Games have done a great job in shining a spotlight on this issue and bringing more women into the industry. We hope this book also helps to show how diverse and inclusive the industry is and encourage more women to consider gaming as a career.

PAC-MAN was among the games that changed the global gamer profile, as it was the first to interest the female population. It became a TV series in 1982 produced by Hanna-Barbera, and the success of that show inspired producers to think about bringing other popular gaming characters to the small screen.

Today, all ages and demographics play, but there are nevertheless interesting gender differences in player profiles. In terms of devices and playing time, younger males typically play on a console for an average of seven to ten hours per week, whereas women are more likely to play on their mobile phones and dip in and out, playing for twenty or thirty minutes at a time.

For women, gaming is more of a social phenomenon, through which they interact usually with a small group of friends, whereas (young) males are more likely to play multiplayer games with large groups of strangers as well as friends. When we look at the detail of who is spending money, and so essentially supporting the industry, it is still largely the younger male demographic that dominates.

Gamers might be thought generally to be indoor types or those less comfortable with 'real' social interaction. This is also largely a myth. The reality is that all kinds of people are gamers, so it would be hard to define the typical gamer.

ULTIMATE GAMER **ALL-ROUND** ENTHUSIAST **CLOUD** GAMER **CONVENTIONAL** PLAYER

HARDWARE ENTHUSIAST **POPCORN** GAMER **BACKSEAT** VIEWER **THE TIME** FILLER

Gamer types

People watch films, like music or read books; these media attract all types of people, and gaming is exactly the same.

As Phil Spencer stated:

'We shouldn't talk about gamers. There's no such thing as gamer, non-gamer. We're all humans. We're just people who like to play. We do not call ourselves a filmer or musicer, so why should we try to define a gamer? Gamers are people.'

Significantly, the distinction between gamers and non-gamers is becoming blurred as non-gaming experiences, such as virtual concerts and fashion shows, are increasingly integrated into games. According to Newzoo, 50% of Gen Z, 37% of Millennials and 28% of Gen X players enjoy hanging out in game worlds without actively playing games, and 70% of Gen Z players, 63% of Millennials and 53% of Gen X players say they will hang out in virtual game worlds without playing in the future.[11] Many of these more casual experiences will happen in the metaverse, and according to Matthew Ball, CEO of Epyllion, we are already playing and hanging out in the major metaverses of the future: *Fortnite*, *Minecraft* and *Roblox*.

Rapid growth in developing countries

Gamers are everywhere, in all corners of the planet. Around half of the world's gamers are in Asia – partly because video gaming originated there and partly because of the sheer size of its market. According to Newzoo, China and the US have the most gamers with 742 million and 197 million players, respectively.[12]

In terms of growth, however, the popularity of gaming is increasing most rapidly in developing countries. Africa and India are seeing high growth in gaming numbers, and areas such as the Middle East are also experiencing a boom in player numbers. Not surprisingly, gaming is a global business. While the Asia-Pacific region dominates sales, many gaming companies are turning to the West for growth, as well as continuously pushing into developing countries, where internet and mobile phone penetration is rapidly opening up access to new markets.

As part of the UN study on climate change, 'The Peoples' Climate Vote', Playmob investigated mobile gaming in countries we had never been into before, like Djibouti, Kyrgyzstan, Sri Lanka and Panama. It was unknown whether there was a volume of active gamers there, but we were astonished at the number of people found playing. The free-to-play model has taken down barriers to play and made gaming affordable for anyone with a device and connection.

Less violence, more exploration

Compared with just a decade ago, when the range of games available was severely limited, there is now a constantly increasing diversity of genres – from action and adventure to sport, from word games, puzzles and quizzes to role-play and simulation – as games companies aim to appeal to an ever-broadening range of demographics. How and what we play also changed throughout the pandemic.

In a 2021 article published by *Sage Journals*, Matthew Barr and Alicia Copeland-Stewart reported the results of an online survey they had undertaken during the Covid-19 pandemic.[13] Respondents most commonly reported an increase in multiplayer gaming, although the move to multiplayer is also associated with a shift to playing online. Many players said they switched genres.

Players also reported a new appreciation of more relaxing, comforting or passive games, related to a reduced interest in competitive or antagonistic mechanics. Players noted that they are 'more likely to play games from less violent genres'. Hinting that the wane in appeal of certain genres was a direct result of the pandemic, one respondent remarked, 'I don't enjoy playing violent games anymore. The world is already scary enough'. To a lesser degree, players expressed an increased desire for games featuring exploration.

The most popular genre of game on mobile is casual, followed by puzzle, then role playing games (RPGs). This can be validated by the number of downloads of hit mobile games in 2022. *Subway Surfers* is the most downloaded mobile game. In 2022, it reached around 300 million unique downloads. This is followed closely by *Garena Free Fire*, *Stumble Guys*, *Roblox* and *Candy Crush*.

Subway Surfers

Mobile games are driving growth

'Gaming has the ability to connect people all over the world with the relevant information they want for incredibly low cost.'
— Marc Merrill, Co-chairman, Co-founder, Riot Games

Recent years have seen a significant shift in gaming platforms away from personal computer (PC) and console towards mobile phones. Consoles have become relatively expensive, while PC games require considerable bandwidth – and a good spec computer to have a good quality game. There are fewer of those challenges with mobile gaming, where file sizes are much smaller and the basic equipment is inexpensive. Not surprisingly, therefore, 2022 saw over 25% growth in mobile gaming popularity, while mobile gaming accounted for 45% of total video gaming revenue worldwide.[14]

Mobile gaming facts:

- In 2021, there were 3.9 billion smartphone users worldwide.[15]
- Players downloaded 82.98 billion mobile games in 2021.[16]
- 79% of people under twenty-two years old play only mobile games.[17]

PC and console gaming facts:

- The global console gaming market was worth $34 billion in 2019 and is projected to reach over $50 billion by 2027.[18]
- In 2020, there were an estimated 1.75 billion PC gamers worldwide, compared with 1.5 billion in the previous year.[19]
- Almost 30% of female gamers play on console or PC every day.[20]
- The most popular PC games are in the war, shooting and survival categories,[21] and include *Call Of Duty: Modern Warfare 2*, *Roblox*, *The Sims 4*, *Overwatch 1&2*, *Minecraft*, *Fortnite*, *League of Legends*, *Counter-Strike: Global Offensive*, *Valorant* and *Grand Theft Auto V*.[22]

Interestingly, console games are more popular in the West than in Asia, where the great majority of gamers play on their mobiles. Established games originally exclusive to PC (and better suited to the larger-screen format) are now appearing in mobile versions.

In recent years, one of the most marked evolutions has been the migration away from boxed retail products towards downloadable digital content (DLC). In 2017, just 21% of all computer and video games sold in the US were in physical format, down from 80% in 2009.[23]

This shift in how we play could give us false illusions of a greener and cleaner industry. Moving from a boxed product and using less plastic and shipping is a step in the right direction, but the industry is consuming massive amounts of energy (charging devices, storing data, servers, etc). However, it is aware of this impact on the planet, and we talk later about initiatives set up to tackle the growing carbon footprint of the industry.

The rise in gaming does not necessarily indicate an increase in physical inactivity. There are now several games that get people moving, such as *Wii Sports* or *Pokémon Go*, using augmented reality (AR) to get them outdoors. In fact, John Hanke, who founded Niantic to create *Pokémon GO!*, set up the game with the aim of making people healthier and happier by getting them outdoors and exploring:

> 'We measure the distance that our users walk, the number of places that they visit and the number of social interactions they have through the game. The theory is that people are out of their house, not watching TV. They're walking through the park, they're exploring the city and there's a positive impact on people's connection with the place they live, with their community.
>
> 'If you spend time in the park, you're more likely to care about it. You're more likely to want to volunteer to clean it up. You may meet your neighbours, you may form community bonds. I really think that if you can encourage people to take a thirty-minute walk every day, it could change the world. They don't need a game to do it, but if we can nudge them

towards that, there's a massive opportunity
to fundamentally improve people's quality
of life.'

Niantic games also require players to explore villages and towns and learn about their history, while other games take the 'escape room' concept out into the real world and have gamers literally following clues to solve a problem. Not only do they get fresh air and exercise while playing, but they often also dress up in appropriate outfits, such as mad hatters and white rabbits for *Saving Alice*, so that the game becomes a fun family outing. Such games sometimes involve non-traditional techniques such as blowing into your phone or putting your hand on the camera to measure your heart rate, which can serve to amuse as well as de-stress.

Finally, of course, there are those who prefer to watch games on platforms such as Twitch and YouTube, rather than actually playing them. Watching games is now one of the most popular types of content on YouTube. Some YouTube influencers also require audiences to get moving, by doing twenty sit-ups or push-ups every twenty minutes, for example.

The way people play games is constantly evolving as technology makes possible what might only have been imagined a few years ago. Much of what we will see change in the next few years may not be what we play or the technology it is on, but the way in which we interact with variations of the same content.

Playing has reached the tipping point

'Gaming has become a mainstream activity for hundreds of millions of people, even if many of them don't consider themselves "gamers", and it's been wonderful to see how gaming has evolved to become one of the most important forces in mainstream culture.'
  — Matt Fischer, Apple's Vice President of the App Store

In her 2011 book *Reality is Broken*,[24] Jane McGonigal reported that, globally and collectively, we were spending 3 billion hours per week playing games. If we could get to 21 billion hours, she argued, we could start to solve some of the world's greatest problems, such as poverty, climate change and obesity (we'll come back to this challenge later in the book).

We have now reached that target: the world's 3 billion gamers are spending an average of 8.6 hours per week playing video games.[25] We have also reached the tipping point of games becoming a serious contender in solving some of the global challenges we face today. The purpose of this book is to inspire the industry to do more and leverage this superpower as a force for good, and encourage those not in the industry to view games in a new and good light.

Gaming facts:

- The average gamer is spending 8.6 hours per week playing video games, which equates to roughly 1.2 hours per day.[26]

- On average, gamers play two to five mobile games a month.[27]
- Gen Z and Millennials spend more time gaming than on any other form of entertainment.[28]

Humans like to play

'It makes you happy, it makes you smile, it makes you want to succeed in a place where you can succeed and not in a place that you are failing. It gives you something new in your life. This is something we discovered very soon that we never thought we would.'
— Robert Antokol, Founder and CEO, Playtika

There are a number of reasons people play games. As well as those who want their games to be competitive and even combative, there are others who play for relaxation, nostalgia or social interaction with games such as *The Sims, Subway Surfers, Roblox, Pokémon GO, Clash of Clans* and *Animal Crossing*.

Play is an innate human need – one that gaming naturally taps into. As Matt Fischer points out, 'Play is an important aspect of life, and we like to provide these fun moments of escape and entertainment alongside advancing humanity through technology.'

Video games are interactive, which means that they give players agency.[29] They foster feelings of competence (or efficacy) and autonomy, which, according to self-determination theory (SDT), are two of humans' three basic psychological needs.[30] They empower players to adopt roles, confront challenges, make choices, get feedback and explore consequences in an engaging and often social context. They enable players to progress at their own pace and fail in a safe environment.

People are motivated to play for a variety of reasons. They may play the same game, but some do so to relax, some to escape, some to feel challenged. People also enjoy problem solving and learning, which many games involve. As we will see (in Chapter 4), this can have positive health benefits. Increasingly, games are being seen as a way of socialising, especially for people who cannot meet up physically.

Most importantly – and this is a theme we will be returning to throughout this book – they enable people to make a difference in virtual and potentially real-world environments. As the game industry is discovering, people love to do something in the virtual world that has an impact in the real world.

Gamers want to do good

'More and more customers are buying into products that they feel represent them and are as much a social statement as a product.'
— Phil Spencer, CEO, Gaming at Microsoft

What players want depends on their motivations to play games they are drawn to. The 'Green Game Jam Player Survey 2022' (we will be talking more about that, too), organised by Playmob and the Playing for the Planet Alliance, shows that gamers want more purpose to their playing – the feeling that they are doing something positive.[31] They also want more decency in terms of game content, to play in and create worlds which are fair and fun for all. There is perhaps a rather 'protestant' sense of guilt at spending so much time playing, which can be offset by doing good in the game. Again, this is a theme we will be returning to.

This good might take the form of designing an interior, saving worlds, leading your clan to safety or word games with your family 10,000 miles away. It might involve helping to save the planet and everything which relies on the planet for survival. Suddenly, our fictional virtual heroes begin to transcend into real heroes as we leverage the power and culture of gaming to play to save the world.

Summary

- Games are commonly misunderstood – no longer are they targeting teenage boys in their bedrooms playing wargames. Gaming is for everyone.

- Games have gone mainstream and reach all types of people, globally.

- Developing parts of the world are some of the fastest growing markets for gaming, due to increasing access to the internet and smartphones.

- Mobile is the number-one platform of choice, but PC is growing again thanks to Steam and other platforms.

- We have gone past the 21 billion hours per week of play time tipping point and now is the time to start recognising real-world action from our gaming efforts.

- People play for a number of reasons now: to escape, to socialise, to realise ambitions to save the real world.

2
An Industry Like No Other

'People can be activated about their passions
much more easily through gaming than by
other industries.'
— Oliver Miao, Executive Advisor, Pixelberry

The games industry is not just the fastest-growing
entertainment industry, it also has greater potential reach, influence and power than any other. In fact,
video games have changed the way that many other
forms of media, from music to film, are produced
and consumed.

In this chapter, we look at the make-up of the industry and how it is developing, the standards and codes
of practice that are guiding that development, how
both profit and non-profit organisations are realising
the industry's potential, and why gaming is uniquely
positioned to be a force for good in the world.

Bigger than film and music

'Gaming has the ability to connect people all over the world with the relevant information they want for incredibly low cost.'
— Marc Merrill, Co-chairman, Co-founder, Riot Games

The games industry is now three times larger than the film and music industries combined in terms of revenue. As we have seen, its total earnings in 2022 from game sales and downloads and in-app purchases were around $184 billion,[32] and that doesn't include advertising revenue. This figure is predicted to grow to $372bn in 2023.[33]

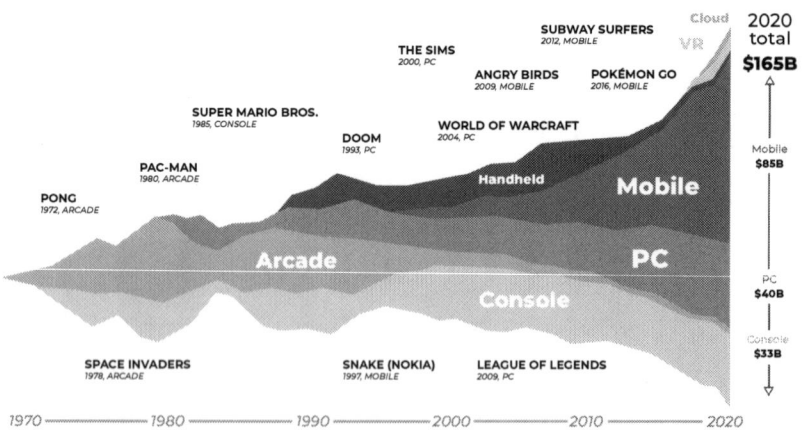

The rise of gaming revenue (Source: Visual Capitalist)[34]

This rapid growth is largely due to the diversification of the industry. Having started off mainly on PC, it then went to console and mobile, and now there are AR and virtual reality (VR) games, not to mention the metaverse as we're entering this era of Web3. This expansion has gone hand in hand with the worldwide increase in internet access and smartphone affordability, which we described in Chapter 1.

Like most other technology-based industries, gaming was started by individual developers (indies); and there are still thousands of indie producers – more than ever, in fact, since almost anyone can develop a game and self-publish it on multiple platforms. As Matt Fischer comments, 'People are surprised to hear that more than 90% of all developers on the App Store are small developers.' Some of these indies are making tens or even hundreds of millions of dollars from their games but, inevitably, the big players – Microsoft, Sony, Activision Blizzard, Tencent and the like – are attracted to them and acquire them to become part of the larger group.

For example, the best-selling video game of all time, *Minecraft*, was started by Markus Persson, known as Notch, who was based in Sweden.[35] When it exploded, he sold it to Microsoft for $2.5 billion. *Subway Surfers*, the most downloaded game in the world, was developed by SYBO in Denmark. The company was sold in 2022 to Miniclip whose main owner is Tencent.[36] Zynga, the creator of *Farmville*, was acquired by Tencent,[37] and even giants are acquiring giants, such as Microsoft acquiring Activision Blizzard (although at the time of writing this book, the deal is not yet finalised).[38]

The best experience for all

'Games are a form of media in the same way that books, radio and TV are. Video games in particular are a powerful way to connect people.'
— Marc Merrill, Co-chairman, Co-founder, Riot Games

Since the days of Nintendo and the Xbox versus Play-Station wars, which superseded games such as *Mario* and *Sonic the Hedgehog* (themselves outgrowths of *Space Invaders* and *PAC-MAN*), devices and games have become ever more sophisticated. For example, it is now possible to play a game on one device (say, a console), and then pick it up on another (eg, your computer or mobile phone).

It seems that so far, every ten years or so there has been a jump in terms of the type and quality of games that come on to the market. As we have seen, mobile gaming is the big thing at the moment, but another jump is in the offing, which is likely to be related to the metaverse, even more cross-platform play or versions of extended reality. However, the future of 'what's next' in gaming is hard to predict and much of what we will see is existing intellectual property (IP) used in different ways, for example, mobile games being used for eSports and advances in speed and interoperability.

As the real and virtual worlds become increasingly indistinguishable, the challenge will be to merge them in a safe, healthy and beneficial way. Many players, for example, are put off VR games because they make them physically sick. Google Glass failed largely as a result of consumer concerns over its actual and potential effects, although Google Glass 2.0 is making a comeback and perhaps there will be a different reaction today.[39]

From the players' point of view, there is a desire to have better and better experiences. For the developers, it is a case of offering players the best experience possible – and retaining them by keeping them engaged, and spending, as long as possible.

Protecting players

Where initially the gaming industry was something of a Wild West, it is now subject to a variety of standards and regulatory codes and guidelines. Co-founder of Hiro Capital Sir Ian Livingstone says:

> 'The games industry, like the film industry, has a rating system for a reason. *Grand Theft Auto*, a massive, huge British success story generating a billion dollars in three days, should be celebrated for its intersection of art and technology and enabling people to play or experience this incredibly immersive world, but it's eighteen rated and children shouldn't be playing that game.
>
> 'It should be celebrated for what it is.
>
> 'While films don't get criticised in that sense, I would say there's a lot more violent films

proportionate to violent games; 95% of games content is actually family friendly. Not enough people know about that, so *games have always been criticised because people just do not understand what is so great about them* [authors' emphasis].'

Back in 1993, the public face of the industry was *Mortal Kombat* – a martial arts combat game in which two players would pummel each other until one was sufficiently stunned to be delivered a 'Fatality' move. Here, the other would grab their opponent's head and rip their spinal cord out of their still standing body. Not surprisingly, parents, teachers and politicians were horrified. The US Congress held hearings about the game and its influence on youth and, as a result, created the Entertainment Software Rating Board, which today rates games based on their age appropriateness.

In Europe, these ratings are known as the Pan-European Game Information (PEGI) system, which has five categories:

- PEGI 18 – suitable for ages eighteen+

- PEGI 16 – suitable for sixteen+

- PEGI 12 – suitable for twelve+

- PEGI 7 – recommended for ages seven+

- PEGI 3 – recommended for ages three+

Of course, not all parents pay attention to these ratings and there is still some educational work to be done to ensure that they are respected.

There are also industry bodies such as the UK's Independent Game Developers' Association (TIGA) and UK Interactive Entertainment (UKIE), which lobby government on behalf of their members in both their and players' interests. These bodies are helping studios to become greener as well (a topic we will be looking at in Chapter 8). UKIE, which is a member of the Playing for the Planet Alliance (we will explain more about that in Chapter 6), has recently created a Code of Conduct for green gaming[40] along with its Sustainable Group that gathers regularly online to discuss and share green gaming practice.

With the advent of the General Data Protection Regulation (GDPR) and Web3 (decentralised ecosystems based on blockchain technology), there will undoubtedly be further improvements in the policing of the gaming industry, in line with all other entertainment businesses, but already the industry is quite savvy in terms of protecting its players. Games companies want to be commercial, but not to the detriment of players – and particularly young people. They can, for example, detect whether a player is spending more than an acceptable amount of time or money in a particular game; if so, the player will be told to 'take a break' or 'go for a walk' or even 'switch off the console' (and they won't be able to switch it on again for a certain amount of time). More companies should do that.

Influencing the real world

'Play has been an innate human need from the beginning of time. Gaming is just the most modern version of that, but we have a great responsibility because, through the power of connectivity, we can reach literally everybody.'
— Phil Spencer, CEO, Gaming at Microsoft

The phenomenal growth of the games industry has made other industries, as well as non-profit organisations, sit up and take notice. Unilever, for example, has been exploring ways to utilise games for its brands, including reaching young people to help them boost their body confidence and self-esteem with its cleansing and moisturising range Dove.[41] Many other brands are working on bringing gaming in-house as it is so strategic to their businesses, including AB InBev, Nike, Adidas, Puma, Red Bull, PepsiCo, Manchester City, KFC and Pizza Hut. Even eyewear retailer Zenni stated that it would have to bring someone in-house to manage its efforts in eSports.[42] Zenni creates a line of blue-light blocking gamer glasses and even has its own X (formerly known as Twitter) feed separate to its main brand account to communicate to its gaming audience.

Fortnite and Heinz have recently teamed up to raise awareness of falling levels of soil quality due to over-farming.[43] Heinz has created a map within *Fortnite* representing one of its own tomato farms, which will educate players on the issue while providing some science, technology, engineering and mathematics (STEM) training. The map will feature greenhouses where young tomato plants are first raised before heading to the fields, where they will grow up to be made into tomato ketchup! The initiative will also raise awareness of the sustainability efforts of Heinz, which has committed to 100% sustainably grown tomatoes for ketchup globally by 2025 and net zero carbon emissions by 2050.[44]

As part of its Pride celebrations in 2021, SYBO teamed up with Lady Gaga's Born This Way Foundation, taking part in the foundation's #BeKind21 event, focused on improving mental health through kindness.[45] To this end, *Subway Surfers* released game character Cleo and a social campaign calling players to practise an act of kindness each day, contributing to the event with 705,000 pledges to be kind. In the first week of the event, *Subway Surfers* saw a 33% increase in impressions and a 7% increase in downloads compared with the previous week.

Subway Surfers: Play with a kind heart

Gaming is attracting big names in the fashion sector, too. Brands such as Burberry and Balenciaga are making a beeline for the more popular games and offering in-game merchandise. In a virtual world, players can be anyone and anything they want. If they want to be head to toe in luxury gear, they can. Balenciaga teamed up with *Fortnite* to sell in-game items, making them affordable with the price tag between $2 and $12.[46] This also gave the brand access to 350 million gamers.

Dior teamed up with *Gran Turismo 7* and introduced a whole new genre to luxury fashion.[47] Gucci has taken up a permanent residence within Roblox by opening up Gucci Town, which sells items such as the Dionysus bag for $4,000.[48] Where formerly such an item could only be used in the game for which it was purchased, Web3 technology has enabled players to use or wear it in other games as well, which increases its 'value'. This can sometimes lead to extreme behaviour, where a virtual bag, for example, sells for more than a real one, as players seek to show off to other players and keep up status.

The brands, too, make more money, since they can claim royalties each time a virtual item is sold on – unlike a real one – and, of course, virtual products don't wear out. There is much debate about non-fungible tokens (NFTs), which are generally created using the same type of programming used for cryptocurrencies. In simple terms, these cryptographic assets are based on blockchain technology. They cannot be exchanged or traded equivalently like other cryptographic assets, such as Bitcoin or Ethereum. Are they just glorified Jpegs or do they offer a great solution to recognise the original creator and leave no ambiguity about an item's history forever?

As in movies, product placement and in-game advertising can be done well or not so good. An example of the latter was the game *Call of Duty: Black Ops Cold War*, where during a stealth mission in East Berlin, while players were infiltrating the German Democratic Republic via train, there was a Doritos poster plastered on the wall. Although the game was designed with the era in mind, Doritos didn't go global until the nineties and this scene took place much earlier than that.

Non-profits are also increasingly seeking to engage with gamers, as they see this as a good way of raising both awareness and funds. Again, if this is done in a rather crass, 'greenwashy' way, players will see straight through it. The other issue here is, because of the opportunity, games studios can be bombarded with inbounds and requests from non-profits. This, of course, takes time on the part of the non-profit and leaves studios not knowing what and who to support. A studio would tend to support a cause which 1) is in reaction to something, ie, the 2023 earthquakes in Turkey and Syria, 2) comes via a close contact who recommends a cause to support, 3) is supported by the board or senior management (top down) or 4) is decided upon by employees (if such a way of working exists in the studio).

When there's a shared alignment of values, there is a positive uplift. Creative Mobile Games' partnership with PlanetPlay will see the developer introduce the first all-electric vehicle into hit mobile racing game *Nitro Nation*. Proceeds raised via sales of the new in-game vehicle will be donated directly to the Hongera Clean Cookstove project in Kenya. This project supports the distribution of 150,000 efficient stoves to rural Kenyan families and will mitigate more than 1.7 million tons of CO_2 over the project's lifetime.[49] Not only will this item sale make a positive impact via giving back to green projects, but it also shows signs of 'normalising' green solutions in-game and promoting electric vehicles.

In later chapters, we will be looking at how the popularity of gaming can be exploited by both businesses and non-profits – sometimes working together – in meaningful and positive ways. If the recipe is right, it can work powerfully for all three parties – games companies, other businesses and/or IP, and non-profits – while also benefiting players, who are in the middle of it all. The industry moves quickly, so we can give good examples of the way it is now, but with the caveat that much is being learned. Our next book will build on this!

To date, Jude's company Playmob has carried out two studies which highlight where the industry has been generating impact. The first, the Playing for the Planet report in 2019, included an assessment of about 260 games studios, which got the Playing for the Planet Alliance off the ground (see more in Chapter

6). It showed the impact games were already having in relation to the UN's SDGs and revealed that the industry was having the greatest impact in the areas of health and wellbeing, the planet and education. These were the most popular global goals that studios were supporting, and this gave great evidence for organisations outside the industry of the areas games were likely to support. We will show this later in the book.

The second study, The Peoples' Climate Vote, was done with the UN itself (see Chapter 5) and driven via a playable advert launched in thousands of games in over fifty countries. The study, an assessment of how people in these countries around the world felt about climate change, ended up being the largest ever on climate attitudes, reaching 33 million people. The results were circulated among world leaders to inform policy on climate change.

A second version was created for the G20[50] and the data was also used for the IPCC report in 2022.[51] For the first time ever, gamers were being viewed as people with opinions and the data collected from them was being used for important policy changes and insights on climate change. Volumes of gamers' voices were heard to influence critical global decisions about our planet.

Playmob has since used a similar approach with other non-governmental organisations (NGOs), such as water and energy companies – an illustration of the increasing influence of gaming in every domain and across sectors and global challenges.

Phenomenal reach and speed

'People are seeing games as a medium that you can take seriously. It's interesting as an experience first, and then the message itself is responsible and is dealing with serious issues in the same way that a well-crafted film might.'
— John Hanke, CEO, Niantic

It is not only the size of the games industry that is a powerhouse for change; it is also its engagement of players. In contrast to some other activities, such as watching TV, gaming is totally engaging (it's tough to multitask while playing a mobile game, since concentration is the key to winning). This means that games hold a lot of attention – and with it a lot of power.

Another factor in the power of gaming is the speed at which people can be reached. Gaming is one of the fastest ways to reach people in all corners of the planet. In a recent research project we conducted on Green Gaming content, we were able to get 389,000 responses in a matter of months. For the UN study mentioned above, we at Playmob reached 33 million people in three weeks. One brand representative commented that games achieved for them in one month the same results as it had taken them fifteen years to achieve!

With an industry of such a vast size, and total engagement and phenomenal speed at our fingertips, comes a big responsibility – a responsibility both to do the right thing and to do things that other industries cannot. It is up to both the industry (and those who are and want to collaborate with the games industry) and the players to recognise that responsibility and make sure they are not doing the wrong thing for people on this planet. We have a choice to do good or not – and it is a vital one, as we shall see.

When you have the choice, choose right.

Summary

- The games industry is three times larger than film and music combined.

- What we play won't change a great deal, but how we play / watch people play will.

- Gaming experiences will advance greatly in the coming years due to advancements of technology.

- Safety and security is a critical factor within the industry, which must be constantly improved and evolve over time as new platforms unfold during Web3.

- The industry will grow with collaborations from outside, such as with NGOs, brands and IP.

- The industry can engage deeply with players, more so than any other form of media which exists on the planet.

3
A Playground For All

'When people connect to something they relate to and they see it in the form of entertainment, it really means something to them. It's a real personal moment as well. There's no one else watching and nothing to get embarrassed about.'
— Oliver Miao, Executive Advisor, Pixelberry

In the previous two chapters, we looked at what gaming is today, how and why, and the phenomenal growth of the industry in the last decade or so. Here, we want to show how gaming culture has evolved. It can now reach places and people it originally had no idea it could include or influence – to such an extent that it is in a position to have a positive impact not only on the world's population, but also on the planet we live on, in ways that previously we could never have imagined.

Over the years, games have moved from being largely single-player to multiplayer, but even single-player games now have multiplayer and social aspects to them – which means that gaming has truly become a playground for all. Gaming today is inclusive and accessible, and the more technology improves, the more people will have access to gaming devices of all kinds. This means one thing – no barriers and borders, leading to more global collaboration, bringing people of all different backgrounds together around a shared interest and common goals. This is hugely exciting when we think about the global problems our world needs to address, as we can really start to grasp the potential gaming has to take quick action at scale.

However, with such openness and accessibility, we must be extremely mindful of security and protecting our players. This is an obligation the industry must work hard to fulfil, for all players everywhere.

Games without borders

'It's about finding connections between people who maybe in the real world would never find each other, because of the geographical or political or religious or socioeconomic barriers that are all around us today. Gaming breaks down so many of those things.'
— Phil Spencer, CEO, Gaming at Microsoft

Whatever social and technological barriers to gaming there might once have been, these have been progressively eroded. Today, anyone with a smartphone – old or young, rich or poor – can play anywhere. During the Covid-19 pandemic, people even donated their old consoles to those who had none, who were elderly or isolated, to help them be entertained and socialise, connecting young and old through gaming.

As Phil Spencer puts it, 'Gaming is a great place for people to hear or feel voices and emotions from people everywhere. I love the diversity of creators and players, the diversity of thought and experience as well as the more traditional kinds of diversity.'

The latest business models such as free to play, where you can download a game to your mobile free of charge, allow people to play without paying a penny. They simply watch ads instead of spending cash. A recent report from Tapjoy found that over 50% of mobile gamers prefer ad-supported games.[52] For brands, governments and NGOs alike, this affords opportunities to reach players at scale to engage in two-way conversations, deliver serious messages in an engaging and entertaining way, and inspire actions that will impact both people and the planet.

The modern world is divided into countries and states, separated by borders. Sadly. Gaming, in contrast, creates a single unified world; a world for everyone everywhere. Of course, there are certain language barriers, but games can also break these down by automatically detecting the language you want to play in and allowing others playing in different languages to join you. Alternatively, you can use the game to improve your foreign language skills.

Games are about playing together. They are a shared experience, where no one is judged on the basis of who they are or where they live or what language they speak (or don't speak), what culture or religion they belong to or any other potentially divisive criteria. People come together all over the world who would not otherwise have done so and consequently learn about each other's cultures and skills; social barriers are broken down and cultural borders disappear.

Games celebrate diversity and aim to be inclusive for all. This is even fed into design principles, as Rachel Franklin, Senior Vice President (SVP) of Positive Play at Electronic Arts (EA), describes:

'A priority for our team has been making our games as inclusive as possible. We know our developers want to build games and experiences that are as diverse as our player community. The concept of inclusive design is a guiding principle that encourages us to consider how gender, age, sexuality, ethnicity, socio-economic background, culture and customs, body shapes and sizes, religious beliefs and other characteristics shape the way we interact with the world, and asks how we might take that insight and better reflect it in our storytelling, characters and the worlds we create. To do this, we support connecting our game developers to consultants who have a deep understanding of certain cultures and societies, to make sure we are getting representation right in our games.'

You don't even have to play games to enjoy the benefits of gaming. Whole ecosystems and communities are building up around games and attracting creators and entrepreneurs. As Ilkka Paananen, CEO and Co-founder of Supercell, explained:

'If you think about games, they are not just games or products anymore; they are ecosystems providing opportunities for the larger community as well. For example, our latest game, *Brawl Stars*, has a massive ecosystem of content creators around it, and lots of people these days make a living on that. It's not just the game, but it's the community, it's the eSports events, all the YouTubers and so forth. Gaming supports entrepreneurship in different countries in a way you would never expect. It's pretty amazing that games can drive those types of things!'

For some, gaming has provided a safe haven, a place where they feel at home, and in turn has boosted confidence. Being dyslexic, Rob Small, President and Co-founder of Miniclip, told us he found gaming to be somewhere he could go and not be judged, be on the same playing field as everyone else. This discovery of gaming also defined his career and life, leading to him building a successful studio on the premise that games should be free and available for everyone, 'unleashing the gamer in everyone'. He was ahead of his time, starting Miniclip in 1999. In 2015, Tencent took a majority stake in the business.

Rob's story is not a one-off, it is true of many who play and work in the industry. Discovering the magic of gaming through looking for a safe place, a place to fit in, is something we completely understand. Jude got into gaming at a young age, playing with her family, sitting around the Commodore 64 or Spectrum, waiting for it to load and taking it in turns to play single or dual mode. It was a social experience for her family.

When she was seven, her dad passed away and her escape was not only to play, but to build games, to create new worlds. Entrepreneurs want to build a better world than the one they live in, and this is what she did, while using games and their ability to transport her to somewhere else and focus on something else rather than what was happening in the real world at that time.

This kick-started her love for games. She discovered the magic and wanted to build more, and play more. At sixteen, Jude would pretend to be grounded, just to get to the next level and beat Dr Robotnik. At university, she discovered a startup developing games for education. This opened her eyes to a new way of gaming: to play for a reason beyond entertainment. It completely hooked Jude and set her on the path of discovering how to use games for real-world good, to make the real world a fairer place for all, just as it is when we play.

Through gaming, you can build relationships and make new friends all over the world; there are even people who have met and married through gaming. Being for all, though, gaming can also drive negative consequences. This is something that as game designers and developers, we must be even more mindful of as our real lives and virtual lives begin to blur.

Mathias's story is one of evolution with the interactions he had with games. Like other Danes, he grew up playing board games during the dark evenings in the Nordics. His mother inherited one of the first Philips computers which was used for Pong and text-prompted adventures. Later, he and his sister started borrowing his neighbour's Nintendo for Mario Brothers.

For Mathias, playing games was due to curiosity – a break, but mostly to interact with others through multiplayer. Battlechess, Starcraft, Counterstrike. His father managed to secure the first 7.7 modem quite early on, so internet was a thing back then on Svovls-bjergvej. And then, around Y2K, he did submerge for some years into Civilization I and II, as well as Age of Empires.

Since becoming a father, it has only been the mobile titles he finds time for in transit and in between sessions. As with many, as we get busy, the style of play adapts, and mobile games have a time and place for everyone.

Shared interests

> 'Gaming drives social contact between disparate
> groups, enabling people to interact with shared rule
> sets in either a competitive or a collaborative way
> that helps build empathy and affinity.'
> — Phil Spencer, CEO, Gaming at Microsoft

Beyond country and language, games enable you to meet like-minded people, to make a connection through your shared interest in the game – 'Oh, so you play *Subway Surfers*, too…' Through forums such as Discord, you can interact with people with similar interests – while playing your favourite game. Apple, for one, has recently been enhancing Game Center, its gaming social network, to make it easier for users to find their friends in games, compete and compare scores, and play together.

Tamzin Taylor, Head of Google Play Partnerships in Western Europe, comments, 'Games have a very important role to play in supporting social and positive impacts on society, from learning new skills, being exposed to different perspectives, for example via narrative-rich games, to finding common communities of interest.'

For Marc Merrill:

'It's a bridge-building activity across differences.
We've gotten thousands of letters and notes
from people all over the world who have
gone to a different university or school or are
somewhere they don't know anyone and found

that games are the mechanism for them to plug into a community that they can relate to and build friendships with. You could walk around almost any city in the world with a *League of Legends* T-shirt or a Teemo hat on and you'll be stopped by somebody. You may not even speak the same language, but you instantly have this thing that unifies and connects.'

Ilkka Paananen points out, 'The vast majority of the most successful games are inherently social, so you don't play them alone, you play them together with friends and other people.' In a game, you are in it together – just as you are when watching a film or a football match. You share the experience and discuss it with others both during and after it.

Joining a game is like walking into a bar and discovering a group of people who all support the same team as you. You instantly have that thing to talk about. You don't even have to play the game to have an interest in it; you can purely be a spectator, as Ilkka pointed out earlier.

As the story below illustrates, there are so many ways to engage with other people through games – a fact that broadens the whole concept of gaming culture.

For the good of the team

One evening, John (not his real name) was making dinner and calling to his kids upstairs that it would soon be ready. On getting the usual response, 'Dad, we're busy. We're in the middle of something...', he decided to go up and see what they were doing and why they couldn't tear themselves away from it – even for food.

He discovered that they were playing *Fortnite* and, within the game, had created a group that was working together. If they stepped away to have their dinner, they would be letting their online group down. It made John realise that they were actually trying to do something good with a group of people, that the game was a collaborative activity and was teaching them social, team-building and problem-solving skills. Not only did he forgive them for not coming down for dinner, he became really excited by the game and ended up investing in the industry.

Increased accessibility

'Players tell me that the truest representation of themselves is in these borderless shared worlds. Whether it's a physical or mental disability that people have, when they go online, they have a gamer tag, they have an avatar, they have their ability to play and that's the thing that leads to the definition of them. It's not somebody seeing them in a chair or seeing their skin colour or anything else. Gaming can be a safe place for people to experience the world in society, but we need to live up to that as an industry. We have to ensure that we create ramps for everybody.'
    — Phil Spencer, CEO, Gaming at Microsoft

It is estimated that there are now a billion people worldwide with some kind of disability. Unlike many physical games, however, online gaming presents few or no barriers to those with disabilities. Yet, until the late 2010s, most games made little effort to accommodate players with motor, visual or auditory disabilities. Now, as the games companies compete to reach an ever-wider audience, they are focusing their attention on people with disabilities.

For example, *God of War Ragnarök*, released in 2022, includes all kinds of features catering to an array of disabilities, while *Tunic* offers a no-fail mode that removes the physical challenges of combat so that players can focus on exploration and the story. On Xbox and Windows systems, players can activate a feature called Co-pilot that allows them to connect two controllers, which then act as a single device.

Gaming can help those with even severe disabilities. SpecialEffect is a UK charity founded in 2007 that modifies controllers so that anyone can play games. Even those with locked-in syndrome can use their eyes to play – something that has transformed their and their families' lives, because for some, it is the first time a child can play with their parents.

In terms of hardware, Microsoft's Xbox Adaptive Controller was until recently the only fully accessible game controller available, but then Sony launched its Project Leonardo for PlayStation, a fully customisable accessible console game controller – designed and built with the help of the disabled community. (It was tested by SpecialEffect, Stack Up, AbleGamers and other such organisations to ensure that it would work for its intended audience.)

There are even games in development that will enable blind people to play by leveraging echolocation. Games such as *Perception* developed by Deep End Games and *Stifled* developed by Gattai Games use this mechanic. Even if you aren't blind, it would give you a mind-blowing experience and a whole new way to play games.

Rachel Franklin commented:

'We [at EA] have worked hard to lessen the gap between capability and disability by breaking down barriers that prevent play through in-game accessibility features, as well as initiatives such as our accessibility patent pledge. We launched our accessibility patent pledge back in August 2021, giving competitors and developers free access to our accessibility-related patents. More recently in December 2022, we announced a further six patents had been added to the pledge. Our most recent additions cover a machine learning (ML) system which helps improve players' experiences and performance by automatically recommending and applying (if approved by the player) configuration settings based on the player's gameplay style. This allows players with disabilities to discover accessibility settings that best address their needs.'

This is extremely important. As Rachel summed up, 'Our players' day-to-day experiences are often so profoundly different that game-makers may not be fully aware of how best to connect players with the experiences they are creating.'

Beyond the freedom such technology gives people with disabilities are its psychological and emotional benefits. Games can boost confidence by providing an equal playing field for all. They can relax us, lift our spirits, enable us to take out frustrations, challenge us and allow us to make progress, which is something as humans we all strive for. Overall, games enable us to use our minds in other ways, making our brains more dynamic and learning social and complex skills, without us even realising it!

Learn as you play

> 'Players form clans and groups that can consist of many different people from many different countries and different cultures; and hopefully that makes people understand each other better.'
> — Ilkka Paananen, CEO and Co-founder, Supercell

Another positive aspect of gaming is that, in a multiplayer game, the more experienced player will often help the newbie – take them under their wing and teach them the ins and outs of the game. This is fulfilling for both teacher and pupil and enhances the shared experience. Gamers generally are helpful and supportive – even if they really want to win!

This doesn't apply only to massively multiplayer online games (MMOs); it can also happen in simple games such as *Golf Clash* and *Words with Friends*, which 'know' that you are new to them and adjust the level of play accordingly, allowing you to progress at your own pace so that you never feel pressured, frustrated or out of your depth.

In some games, it is possible to shadow an experienced player, eg, by acting as a look-out, while you learn the ropes. Of course, most games have built-in tutorials for those who prefer independent learning or learning from the machine and not a real person.

Safe spaces

'Our games are hopefully role models to our players, and individual studios can be role models to the industry.'
— Oliver Miao, Executive Advisor, Pixelberry

As we have seen, gaming enables players to be whoever they want to be, to take on a completely different persona or a different type of life and to do things they wouldn't do in the real world. This can be really exciting and freeing, but it also carries potential dangers. Gamers can conceal their real identity and exploit that anonymity in negative ways.

This is, of course, part of a wider problem that the internet has caused (eg, fake Facebook or X/Twitter accounts), but gaming is more fully aware of it than many other online activities and is striving hard to limit its damaging effects, working with organisations such as the National Society for the Prevention of Cruelty to Children to protect children in particular. There are, for example, tight controls around chats, so that any suspicious content or activity is quickly spotted. Games can be moderated either manually by a person or using AutoMod, which relies on sentiment analysis, stance and intent detection. AutoMod uses Natural Language Processing (NLP) and ML techniques to understand the meaning and intent of messages to decide if they are harmful.

As Rachel Franklin shares with us:

'An important step in the EA Positive Play journey came in 2020, when the team launched our Positive Play Charter, which restated to our players how to act and engage when they play with other people. It also states our commitment to combat disruptive behaviour and describes what positive behaviour looks like in interactions, experiences and environments. Everyone deserves a fun experience when they play and the charter makes that clear while outlining the action we will take against behaviour or content that breaks the rules.'

Rachel Franklin and the wider EA team have built upon the Positive Play Charter foundations to good effect. Rachel states:

> 'Our players have responded well to it – in fact, around 97–98% abide by the rules. We have seen a decrease in *Apex Legends* club names violating rules and we have also noted that 85% of players who get a warning from us don't repeat disruptive behaviour. Our moderation is done by tech and expert human review, which we will continue to fine-tune as we learn.'

The industry, too, is striving to make gaming a safe space for all. As Matt Fischer comments, 'It's very important to us that the App Store is a safe and trusted place for customers to discover games and make purchases within their games.'

Rachel Franklin goes on to say, 'At EA, I'm proud to lead the Positive Play team that's working hard to make sure that our gaming communities are fun, fair and safe and that our actions match up with our words.'

As with all online activity, parents and guardians have a responsibility to ensure that their children are playing age-appropriate games and playing them safely. It is also important for schools, and society in general, to inform and advise young people in this respect. We must move with the times in terms of education as well as technology. Games studios have a responsibility to protect players, and with more people playing than ever before, governments and charities have an interest in protecting people through games too.

Summary

- There are no borders in games. Anyone can play from anywhere, meaning social games can become rich cultural experiences.

- Games are being built with inclusive design, ensuring that they have the widest appeal to all.

- You don't have to play to be part of the gaming experience; you can watch (gaming is now the most viewed content on YouTube).

- Games are a platform to bring people together, from all walks of life and corners of the planet.

- Accessibility is key – games can open up worlds to those who have disabilities, and the more the industry can take restrictions into account, the more players it can reach.

- Games should be safe spaces, where kindness to others is key. Games companies are taking into account negative behaviours and acting quickly against them so that the majority can have great experiences.

PART TWO
PLAYING FOR OUR LIVES

'There is enormous potential in the models that so many companies are creating to drive positive human behaviours and learning opportunities. Through games, we learn team-oriented values and sportsmanship, how to have healthy competition and how that improves performance. Gaming leverages our intrinsic motivation, with learning as an outcome.'
— Marc Merrill, Co-chairman, Co-founder, Riot Games

Those who don't play games or are unfamiliar with the nature or culture of gaming, which we investigated in Part One, often jump to the conclusion that games are bad for us: that we play too much, that we spend too much on gaming and that the games we play do nothing for our mental, physical or psychological health. Such negative assumptions are, of course, reinforced whenever an unfortunate incident attracts media attention, since the media have always been eager to denigrate new forms of technology and entertainment – from the invention of the printing press to the advent of the internet. In Part Two, we aim to challenge those claims and show that, on the contrary, games are essentially a force for good in the modern world.

In Part One, our goal was to set the scene, show what games are about and the potential upside by thinking of this cultural megatrend as a modern-day superpower. In Part Two, we look more into the question 'Can games be good for us?' and explore some of the key elements of games being a powerful force for good in terms of tools for education, psychologically and as a public service. There are so many examples and the area is such a fast moving one, we have not been able to cover everything, but we have touched on a range of examples to give you a feel for how games can be a force for good.

This section will also act as a precursor to Part Three, in which we examine how we unlock this incredible superpower to solve the world's greatest problems.

4

Can Games Be Good For Us?

'Everyone in the industry knows how powerful games can be in supporting the growth of friendships and building a sense of community.'
— Rachel Franklin, SVP Positive Play, EA

Gaming has variously been linked with sleep deprivation, insomnia and circadian rhythm disorders, with anxiety and depression, and even with aggression. However, it has also been claimed that gaming improves motor skills and muscle strength, encourages the maintenance of healthy weight and promotes appreciation of nature and the environment;[53] that it enhances cognitive function, reduces the chances of our brains deteriorating prematurely, helps us to relax and meditate, and opens up our minds to learning.[54] This in turn represents a new wave of opportunities to provide people with information in such a way as to help them to learn and do something useful with that newly acquired knowledge.

As Joost Vervoort of Utrecht University said, 'Games can and do resonate deeply with people in different ways, individually but also collectively through communal experiences, the building of solidarity, new identities and new shared meanings.'

Gaming is particularly well suited to the elderly and those with limited mobility. For those who are stuck at home (or even in a home) for any reason, gaming is not only a great form of entertainment and an excellent way to keep the brain active, but also a means to connect with friends and relatives they may not otherwise be able to engage with. As the elderly have gained confidence in using technology, they have found gaming to have all kinds of advantages over paper-based entertainments such as puzzle books, crosswords and jigsaws.

As we saw in Chapter 3, gaming has been shown to be a boon for people with all kinds of disability, and yet the negative press persists. Let's look at some of the reasons behind this.

Media image

'Understanding the implications and how to proactively foster good outcomes and mitigate the potential negative outcomes is something we all have a responsibility to do. Why would somebody

treat somebody else poorly online, what are the key
driving factors and what can we do about it?'
— Marc Merrill, Co-chairman, Co-founder,
Riot Games

When books began to circulate among the general
public back in the fifteenth century, it was feared that
they would spread all kinds of evil ideas, take people
out of the real world and into a world of fantasy and
indulgence, leading to general social degradation.
The same thing happened with the advent of the wire-
less and the moving picture and the television and
the internet.

What these phenomena all had in common was a
basic human instinct: fear of the unknown. Anything
new and unfamiliar is always assumed to be a threat
rather than an opportunity or a potential benefit.

Little wonder, then, that the recent growth of
gaming has come under fire from all sides – and that
the flames have been eagerly fanned by the media,
always ready to sensationalise an impending doom. It
is the latest threat to our mental, physical, psychological and social health. It will consume our minds and
energy and destroy civilisation and the planet...

As we have seen in Part One of this book, there is
little evidence that the spread of gaming will have any
of these dire consequences. Nevertheless, it is generally associated with certain negative behaviours that
none of us want to encourage or condone. Gaming is
mostly an indoor activity, and we don't want people
to avoid going outdoors. Games are competitive and
sometimes combative, while we want people to be

collaborative and non-violent. Some games can even be addictive.

We have also seen, however, that gaming is spreading to the real world and even encouraging outdoor activity. We now know that a small portion of games are adult only or involve simulated violence, and that violent games are declining in popularity relative to other types. The vast majority of games in the market today are family-friendly, social games.

Beyond this, we should ask ourselves, 'Does gaming incite violence and lead to addiction or, rather, are people with violent or addictive tendencies attracted to those types of games?' If a person has an addictive personality, they might indeed become addicted to games; but they might just as easily become addicted to TV or drugs or something else. Addiction can, of course, be a product of other things in a person's life: the way they were brought up, their mental state, their personality. Being aware of having an addictive personality is the first positive step to a person ensuring they limit their time on gaming.

It has even been shown that violent games, rather than encouraging real violence, can actually deflect or dissipate it. Christopher Ferguson, a Stetson University psychology professor, is a leading researcher in the field, and his studies – conducted to date over fifteen years – have consistently reported no connection between real-world violence and violent video games.[55] On the contrary, people who play such games typically report that they find them a release, both physically and mentally. Games can relieve stress and anxiety in a safe and controlled way.

Game player forums vs social media

'Games, being interactive, have more emotional connection and that's a real power of them.'
— Oliver Miao, Executive Advisor, Pixelberry

Social media have mushroomed as a means of keeping in touch with friends and family and sharing experiences, and they undoubtedly have their positive aspects. Comparisons with gaming, however, have highlighted the negative side of social media. A 2020 study by GWI found that social media users commonly experienced a whole raft of frustrations, including:[56]

- Bullying, discriminatory or hateful behaviour (32%)

- Lack of real human connection (30%)

- Portrayal of an unrealistic self-image (27%)

In contrast, the same study revealed these positive motivations behind gaming:

- To relieve boredom (61%)

- To have fun with friends and acquaintances (38%)

- To improve skills (37%)

Interestingly, during the Covid-19 pandemic, it was observed that people were increasingly using gaming in preference to social media as a means to communicate and bond with others.[57] Social games such as *Words With Friends* and multiplayer *Sudoku*, whether played with friends and family or with complete strangers, gave them a sense of social fulfilment they did not find through social media.

It is not for us to denigrate social media, which undoubtedly serve a purpose, but scrolling endlessly through other people's lives, knowing that most of what you are seeing isn't 'real', can ultimately be self-defeating – instilling a sense that the instant gratification everyone is seeking is forever just out of reach. Worse, as we know, social media is susceptible not just to boasting, complaining and fake news, but also to bullying and discriminatory or hateful behaviours, not to mention grooming and other criminal acts.

When you interact with people in a gaming environment, there is a focus, a sense of real-time collaborative socialising that can be much more fulfilling. Paradoxical as it may seem, an imaginary game can prove to be more real than the real world as seen through the distorting lens of social media.

Psychological benefits of games

'When you have a community [in gaming], you're solving two things. First, you're making the communication with the player much easier. Second, you're alleviating the loneliness of a lot of people.'
— Robert Antokol, Founder and CEO, Playtika

Much research has been done on the effects of gaming on mental and psychological health – and the results are overwhelmingly positive. In their 2021 article, Matthew Barr and Alicia Copeland-Stewart point to the documented benefits of playing games, such as stress relief, mood restoration, cognitive skills development and the combatting of loneliness, as well as to the mechanisms that cause these effects, including Csikszentmihalyi's flow.[58] This is a state of optimal experience thanks to the balance of challenge versus achievement inherent in video games. Because games ensure that players face challenges that they are able to overcome, they naturally have a positive effect on the players' mood.

The authors' online survey undertaken during the Covid-19 pandemic asked people about their gaming habits and the effects they experienced on their wellbeing. Almost three-quarters of respondents said they had increased the amount of time they spent playing games as a result of Covid restrictions and more than half of them reported an impact on their wellbeing, the overwhelming majority a positive impact.

Ash Brandin, Educator and Innovator, commented:

'One of the biggest benefits of games that we often overlook is their psychological structures that motivate us to begin with. Anything that we enjoy ignites a feeling of intrinsic motivation in us, and that is largely due to three factors: competence, autonomy, and relatedness.'

Whatever you enjoy doing – baking, running, reading – you probably enjoy it for those reasons. It makes you feel accomplished, in control and perhaps socially connected to (or independent from) other people.

Video games ignite these same feelings. We feel a surge of competence when we beat a boss, we feel autonomy and power when we decide what to do in a virtual world, and we may feel connected to other people in the game. When we – and our kids – feel these things for 'good' hobbies, we applaud it. If our kids wanted to draw or paint or play the cello for three hours a day, we'd be thrilled they were so committed to something. As soon as that commitment shifts to video games, it's no longer a 'good' use of time, but psychologically, the draw and the intrinsic motivation are the same.

Some might say that video games draw us in with other things like graphics or sex appeal or weapons, but there are thousands of types of video games in the world and most people only like a small subset. That has to be because it gives them that feeling of intrinsic motivation to make them want to keep playing.

Adam Grant, behavioural psychologist and author, recently commented on gaming, saying:

'Compared to kids who don't play, those who play for three+ hours per day have a better working memory and impulse control. Experiments show cognitive benefits for adults too.'[59]

Another way in which games have a big mental and psychological impact is in inspiring players to explore new interests, even careers, after taking on evocative roles. For example, people want to become city planners after playing *SimCity* or learn to play a real guitar after playing *Guitar Hero*.

As we have seen, gaming also has sociological benefits. A 2018 online Forbes article reported that around two-thirds of gamers claimed to have made up to five friends while playing games, many of them saying they had made even more.[60]

Games to support teaching and training

'People are often intrinsically motivated to engage [with games], and then end up learning – sometimes without even being aware of it.'
— Marc Merrill, Co-chairman, Co-founder, Riot Games

As we saw in Part One, video games have a power of interaction and intrinsic learning built into them like no other medium. Such games are now known as 'serious games' (not a tag we particularly like), but the truth is, games have always been serious insofar as they have a strong teaching element – from the simple days of *Tetris* increasing brain-power through tumbling blocks, to 'edutainment' games like *Donkey Kong Jr Math*, to the thousands of historical details in grand strategy games like *Crusader Kings II*.

What is even more exciting is that today, companies outside the games industry are increasingly wanting to adopt games or game-like principles into their training to make it more engaging, more appealing to younger people. They see this as key to attracting the right talent.

GlassLab's partnership with EA led to the creation of *SimCityEDU*, a game-based classroom tool that uses the popular *SimCity* franchise to engage students in real-world challenges. *SimCityEDU* has been piloted by over 100 teachers and 3,000 students.

Early in our careers, we worked on development projects which linked together games and training to apply real-world knowledge and impact. One example is a project with a global energy company, which was changing its whole ordering process. This meant that lots of different people needed to understand what was happening and why. At the time, management circulated a 1,000-page PowerPoint presentation and hoped that everyone would read it and take it all in, with no way of knowing how much of it was sticking or whether there were any issues that they had failed to address.

The management, however, knew that this kind of training is something games are really good at, that they are the ideal way of showing the difference between what had happened before and what would happen after the change, and the impact it would have. Games can show cause and effect and highlight the roles played by different employees in the process and, mainly, what could go wrong in stages which may not be visible to the employees. By showing their employees these things in a virtual environment which gave real-time feedback, the managers would not only avoid the risk of mistakes being made in the real world, which could be costly for the business, but also involve staff in the process and check that they all understood how and why the change was taking place, aligning everyone.

Another professional training project example involved simulating an emergency, such as a fire, on an oil rig. The game required workers to act as they would in the event of the emergency and allowed them to see whether they survived or died as a result. There were rules and drills to be followed and a time limit to be respected, with the overall aim of getting everyone off the rig safely, so it was very much a team game – with a serious purpose.

Education, too, has been changed by video games through the use of technologies that help teachers and students communicate in new ways. When we started our careers in the games industry about twenty years ago, this was a radically new idea, but now it has spread to all corners of the teaching world.

However, there still has to be careful consideration, as Sir Ian Livingstone states:

'The problem surrounding educational games is that they are often made by non-gamers and they tend to be a bit boring. Whereas the entertainment games are purely for entertainment and tend to be amazing.'

The use of existing games or experienced game creators stepping into education can ensure that educational games are enjoyable and learning actually happens.

Scotland has always been particularly innovative in its thinking about how games can be used to teach more effectively – all across the curriculum. Even back in the 2000s, the Scottish education system had deals with PlayStation and Xbox, which supplied teachers with games and consoles to use in the classroom. Teachers would apply to have a console, and then create case studies of the way they used it to give ideas and inspiration to other teachers who wished to adopt the same approach. Creating case studies meant that teachers could build upon ideas rather than using prescriptive lesson plans.

In one example we were involved in, whole classes of kids were asked to play games – from the 'gifted' and 'talented' ones at the top of the class to those who were behind at the back. The teachers warned us in advance that so-and-so had 'no attention span' and would 'probably last ten minutes'.

As soon as this particular kid started playing, he excelled. He was phenomenal. When the class had to play a game together, he became the leader; and when they were asked to build their own game using simple building block technology, he not only came up with a creative idea, but also made sure that everyone else was included. The teachers were simply blown away: for the first time ever, this boy had sat through an entire lesson – and it went on for two hours. Had they not highlighted him at the beginning, we would have assumed he was a natural creative and leader.

As we said in Part One, gaming creates a level playing field in which everyone is equal.

We discovered that games had the same effect on the teachers, too. Before we went into the classrooms, we brought all the teachers together after school, in the computer lab, to show them how the games worked. Some were excited at the prospect, saying, 'I don't care that my day's finished and I should be going home. This is going to be fun.' Others sat back, arms crossed, and said, 'This is ridiculous. Why are we playing games?' Within fifteen minutes, all of them were enjoying it – especially the people who had thought it ridiculous.

This is the really important thing about gaming culture: the fact that we are all essentially players. We all like to do playful things. The trouble is, we tend to forget that play is such an important part of life. Then, when we get to do it again, it unlocks a part of our brain that gives us real enjoyment. From an educational point of view, these teachers discovered that they could take a popular off-the-shelf game such as *Roblox* or *Minecraft* – a game that is ostensibly for pure entertainment, and one that kids love – and weave their own curriculum and lesson ideas around it.

In Scotland, some primary schools have games consoles in every classroom, being used in different ways depending on the age of the pupils and the curriculum. Primary one (age five) pupils might be using a dance mat to count their steps and creating leader boards that help them learn their numbers. As well as the educational value of the game, there are social benefits, such as learning to take turns and work in teams.

The older kids might be using games like *Guitar Hero* or *Band Hero*, where they would need to collaborate to devise a name for the band, design a logo and write lyrics for the songs, which encourages creativity. Then they would have to create a business plan: how they are going to advertise their gigs and sell tickets, how much profit they might make and what they might spend it on, which would develop their mathematical and practical skills. They might also plan a tour, which would improve their knowledge of geography… all from playing a game.

There are games that help teach languages and other skills. As Jude noted:

> 'My son, who is four, recently said to me,
> "Mummy, I'm going to teach you about yoga."
> He sat me down, put his hands together and
> said, "Namaste." When I asked him how
> he had learned that, he told me it was from
> playing *Lingo Kids* – a series of thirty-second
> games that teach literacy and numeracy in a
> fun way and bring in all aspects of life, from
> cooking to exercise to daily routines.'

The potential for teaching through games is huge, and we are seeing a massive rise in the production of educational games. Whatever the value of this type of gaming proves to be, it is certainly preferable to giving a child a smartphone and getting them to watch a movie.

Games as a public service

'Games are a massive opportunity to make the
world a smaller place.'
— Ilkka Paananen, CEO and Co-founder,
Supercell

An analysis we conducted of over 200 games and
gaming impact initiatives across the industry highlighted its commitment to the UN SDGs, although
this is not always widely appreciated. The UN SDGs
are the most important goals of our time, which aim
to make the world a better and safer place for all by
2030, and we will look closely at these in Chapter 6.
What we discovered in our analysis is that support
is highest for SDG 3, 'Good Health and Well-Being',
followed by SDG 15, 'Life on Land', as shown by the
figure below.

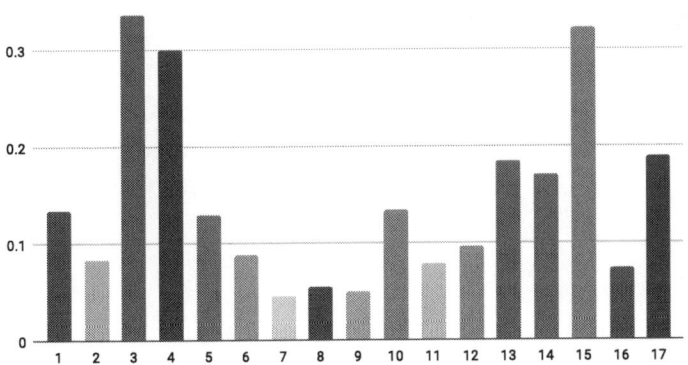

Games industry alignment to SDGs 2019 (Source: Playmob)

Of the industry leaders surveyed for the Playing for the Planet report,[61] the majority agreed that video games can:

- Successfully raise awareness for a cause (96%)

- Assist awareness and learning (87%)

- Drive positive behavioural change (74%)

Of the respondents in this study, 87% intended to run more campaigns and promote key environmental messages, underscoring the need for more refined input from SDG sector experts to focus impacts and highlight successes.

As we are showing, games have a huge opportunity and responsibility to generate real-world impact and can be the most effective public service platform we know to educate, inspire and generate change. If we are to achieve the SDGs by 2030, we need to use platforms and tools that have global scale and can act quickly. Games to date have been misunderstood and the opportunity is now at our fingertips – as well as battling it out to earn extra lives or exclusive content, imagine battling it out to halt climate change and save our planet.

Going green

'Companies are having to be more aware of the impact they're having in the world. At some level, players and shareholders are starting to look at that.'
— Alan Gershenfeld, President and Co-founder, E-Line Media

We have explored how games can be good for us and how their becoming entwined in our daily lives will open up more opportunities for positive impact, but we must be extremely mindful that we don't solve problems while creating even more. Plus, gaming is only going one way – more people are playing and this means the carbon footprint of the industry is rising.

However, this is one area the industry has come together on to take action quickly. As Sam Barratt, Chief of Youth, Education and Advocacy at UN Environment and Co-founder of the Playing for the Planet Alliance, commented about the industry:

'I have three hopes. One, for sustainability to be the default in the sector. Thinking green needs to become normal for everyone, not something that someone in HR does part-time. Two, I'd like the industry to be a pathfinder that others in the tech sector can learn from. Three, I hope the industry keeps learning and testing new strategies so that the power of gamers is harnessed for the good of the planet.'

Electronic waste (e-waste) is one of the fastest-growing waste segments globally.[62] It includes all broken, unusable or outdated/obsolete electronic devices, components and materials. Sadly, though, only sixty-seven countries worldwide have legislation in place to deal with e-waste, and even this legislation isn't all-encompassing with rules that do exist often not enforced. Particularly in many low-income countries in Africa, Latin America and South-East Asia, e-waste isn't a priority on the political agenda.[63]

Yet when you talk to people running a studio about its carbon footprint, the response you are likely to get is, 'Well, we're digital, so we don't have a carbon footprint.' Then you get them to think about everything that they use – energy in the office, transport to and from homes, servers, etc, and they realise that 'digital' doesn't necessarily equate to 'carbon-neutral'.

Gaming also uses a significant amount of electricity, which adds to its overall carbon footprint. The latest generation of consoles consume around 200 watts of electricity during use, placing them at the upper end of household appliances.[64] In the US alone, their use equates to an estimated 24 million tons of carbon emissions every year.[65] Even online games – now, as we have seen, the most popular form of gaming worldwide – require a lot of data usage, contributing to internet pollution, which accounts for almost 3.7% of all global greenhouse gas emissions.[66]

Given the vast number of consoles still purchased each year, a large opportunity exists for the gaming industry to take the lead on developing e-waste education and recycling programmes. So far, though, the uptake has been modest and fragmented, mainly led by individual local councils or games companies. To encourage systems-level change, we need more education around e-waste and policy changes driven by the industry and/or government.

Resources are now starting to become available specifically for the games industry to help it better understand its footprint and how to reduce it. 'A Drawdown-Aligned Framework for the Gaming Industry' was released in March 2023, providing games companies with a comprehensive template to begin their carbon-reducing journeys.[67]

Summary

- Despite historically receiving negativity from the media, the image of gaming is starting to change. We are hopeful that our efforts with this book will help to flip the conversation to shine a new light on games.

- Games can motivate us – they help us feel accomplished, in control and socially connected.

- Games can be more social than social media platforms, combating issues such as loneliness and negative online behaviour.

- Games are increasingly being used in educational and professional training environments, as well as for research purposes.

- The industry has already started generating real-world impact towards the SDGs, according to Playmob's 2019 analysis.

- There is a heightened awareness around the industry's environmental impact, so we must be extremely mindful we do not play to fix a problem while creating another.

5
Levelling Up – Games As A Superpower

'Through a broad-based creator platform, we can help raise different voices, and that's a huge opportunity for our industry that we're just now starting to get our head around.'
— Phil Spencer, CEO, Gaming at Microsoft

We tend to think of games as a one-way process: the gamer deriving enjoyment – and, hopefully, all the other benefits we outlined in the previous chapter – from whatever they are playing. In fact, games are an effective and potentially powerful two-way communication tool – a fact that is only beginning to be appreciated, not only by gamers and the gaming industry, but also by the world at large.

It is an advantage gaming has over other media forms, such as film and television, which are essentially unidirectional and passive forms of communication. As we saw in Chapter 2, gaming is now bigger than those or any other media. This means that it is possible to communicate with people in all corners of the planet, including those who were unreachable before, with the aim of not only selling them products and services via advertising, but also getting their feedback on all kinds of topics and issues.

From the players' point of view, this two-way communication allows them to speak up on things that matter to them – to have their voices heard, from what they want to see more of in their games to how they want to effect change in the real world. As stated earlier, games are an equal playing field with no borders, which means that all 3 billion+ players have the opportunity to speak up. This makes gaming a profoundly important tool for those who are not able or are even afraid to speak up.

Games could also become an important democratic tool. As highlighted by futurist Noah Raford in his 2022 TED talk, games 'are going to become the platform through which tomorrow's social battles will be fought and the source of recruitment for some of the strangest and possibly most impactful social movements of the future.'[68] The speed at which gaming can achieve this is phenomenal. It took television twenty-two years to reach 50 million viewers; *Pokémon Go* achieved this in only nineteen days.[69]

We have experienced this speed of action in our own research and work, from viewing how scientists were able to find solutions in days rather than decades thanks to games such as *Foldit* and in our own work enabling Dove to touch people's lives in months rather than years and supporting UNDP to reach a representative sample of over 50% of the global population in just three weeks. We are only beginning to see the huge potential to level up gamers' voices and actions in this way.

However, it is all very well collecting opinions and information, but what can and should be done with it all, and how? In this chapter, we will explore some of the ways in which this data can be used for meaningful and positive ends; and in later chapters at how gamers themselves can become a force for good by taking direct action to literally change the world.

Listening to gamers

'You've got a lot of engaged users, you've got a lot of eyeballs; you have a big opportunity to put messaging in front of people.'
—John Hanke, CEO, Niantic

As we have shown, gaming is now a uniquely effective way to engage people. Rather than spending big budgets on conventional research to reach a limited sample of a particular population in a matter of weeks or months, organisations can use gaming methodology to achieve a global scale, but still in a scientific way, in a fraction of the time.

In 2019, Playmob was contacted by the UN to discuss gaming and climate action. The message we received was, 'We need to tell the world what nationally determined contributions (NDCs) are, and are hoping you can help.'

Our response: 'What *are* NDCs?' If you haven't heard of them either, NDCs are part of the Paris Climate Change Agreement and specify the efforts each country needs to make to reduce national emissions in line with this agreement.

The team immediately saw the difficulty. Who is going to be interested in NDCs when they have probably never even heard of them? They are certainly not going to read the whole Paris Agreement to find out about it. Then the exam question: how do we ask the global population to speak up on what they care about, and influence and increase the NDCs in their own country by putting pressure on politicians to speed up progress to reducing emissions?

When the team delved a little deeper, we discovered the real problem: a small group of people deep in the detail of climate change solutions. However, this is an issue for the entire global population, and so we needed to know how the world felt and what they wanted, in order to drive real change, and fast. If world leaders were to make the right decisions, they needed the global population to speak up. It was to be nothing less than the biggest study ever conducted on climate attitudes, run in over fifty countries and sampling 56% of the global population, and the data generated would be made available to world leaders to put them in a better position to develop and implement policy around climate change.

It was an enormous challenge – and the results were needed quickly. If the UN were to send a conventional survey via email to that number of people in that number of markets, they would probably achieve a response rate of less than 1%, which was nowhere near enough.

It so happened that the UN's Head of Climate Policy and Strategies, Cassie Flynn, was on the New York subway one morning (the UN is based in New York). While looking around, she observed:

'Everyone had their heads down, staring at their mobile phones. When I looked closer, I realised they were all playing *Candy Crush* or similar games. It was then I realised we need to be communicating to people globally in a medium they are all hanging out in and on their terms – we need to reach them through games!'

It was her 'aha' moment, when she suddenly realised that gaming was the answer. Which is where we came in.

The Playmob team designed a thirty-second interactive advert to place within thousands of mobile games (see 'Playable ads' below). When players ran out of coins or lives, they would be shown a survey in the form of a little quiz game within the advertising space. If players wanted an extra life in that game, they had to open the quiz and answer the questions.

The ad began with the statement, 'World Leaders are listening. Have your voice heard on climate change.' The team made sure players knew that their responses would be anonymous (demographic information was asked for, but never personal details). This was crucial to getting a good response, as players would know that their voice would actually count and at the same time feel protected and safe, even if they voiced potentially controversial or (in their particular political or legal environment) dangerous views. Oxford University had provided the polling rigour and methodology in terms of demographic buckets per market and sampling, so the team had to ensure these parameters were adhered to for the data to be validated.

Playable ads

There is nothing worse in the middle of a game than being 'taken hostage' by an ad. One that you can't even skip. They might help ad agencies with their stats, but they do nothing for the popularity of a game, so game developers may be reluctant to host them.

To be acceptable, in-game ads need to be skippable at some point. The player can choose to watch, in which case they gain the necessary lives or coins to be able to continue the game, or not, in which case they must either wait a certain time before being able to continue or pay to do so.

Mission 1.5 playable advert (Source: Playmob)

Even if an ad is opt-in, it can only be effective if it is watched; if the player uses the duration of the ad to make a cup of tea or feed the cat, its potential value is lost. The advantage of playable ads, from the advertiser's point of view, is that the player has to interact with the ad, so is more likely to absorb its message. From the player's point of view, the potential advantage is that they can learn something or do something useful – as in the case of our ads for the UN survey. World leaders were listening to what mattered to players.

In this case, the questions were around different policies to do with business or agriculture or the oceans, and players were asked to say what they thought or felt should happen in each case. Incidentally, the longest part of the whole process was getting the questions right. The UNDP, to which Cassie Flynn is Senior Advisor, has over 400 climate specialists, each of whom wanted their input into the survey. The questions were also run past Project Draw-down.[70] Even NASA was involved in the process. Then the questions had to be understandable to non-specialists, but gamey and fun to appeal even to the short-attention-span generation.

The methodology had to be exactly right. For this, professional pollsters from Oxford University were involved. They set parameters such as targeting players only once, so there was no double count-ing, and setting specific numbers around obtaining the required demographic quotas in each market – minimum numbers of people in each age group, gender, educational level, etc – to generate properly representative samples.

The next challenge was to reach people in countries which the team had never been in before. Most data gathering had been carried out to date in the US, UK and other parts of Europe, so the big question was, could the platform physically reach people in other areas? Were there enough games and gamers in each market to reach?

We carried out testing in small sampling in ten markets to get an idea of bandwidth and volumes. Fallback rates (the percentage of ads that were not served/seen) were initially high, so we carried out optimising to reduce the file size. This drastically low-ered the fallback rate to ensure we could reach the highest number of people.

After a series of test runs to check engagement rates, the ad was then rolled out to the full fifty-two countries, reaching 33 million people in three weeks. One team member described seeing the numbers mounting as being like watching a horse race, with different 'runners' taking the lead and dropping back. Typically, the eighteen to thirty-five age range buckets filled really quickly, while other demographics, such as the over-sixties in India and those not in education, stayed relatively empty. Once there were sufficient numbers in a bucket, it would close and the focus would switch to filling the other buckets. Fortunately, this strategy worked and there were only a few buckets that didn't completely fill.

After just three weeks, the team had a representative sample of 56% of the global population, which was an unprecedented achievement. The data was then analysed and published as The Peoples' Climate Vote Report.[71] This generated so much interest that the G20 requested its own version of it and the data was used within the 2022 IPCC report.[72] This – the scale, the speed, the accuracy when optimising – was only possible through the power of gaming. It was the first of its kind. Finally, gamers were being recognised as people too!

Hitting the target

'It doesn't matter how great your intentions are if you don't have reach.'
— John Hanke, CEO, Niantic

As we have seen, the UN survey was a targeted approach to obtaining a response from gamers, but the way of targeting can be on the spectrum from specific (even down to postcode) on one side to blanket spread and open on the other. To begin with, we know that different types of people (different age groups, genders, etc) will play different types of games, so we can aim our playable ads at, say, eighteen- to twenty-five-year-olds. We can then restrict our coverage to a particular geographical area – say the southeast of England.

Playmob has delivered this method for organisations and companies. Northumbrian Water, for example, was only interested in the data coming from Northumbria, Essex and Suffolk – in some cases, particular postcode areas – but keeping the demographic targeting open to test who would respond.

Similarly, Unilever wanted to make its Dove Self-Esteem initiative reach more young people globally, to have a positive effect on their lives. This meant targeting a particular age group in certain markets and optimising the playable advert to engage players to the end, ensuring that they would see the messages all the way through. The approach with Dove went under rigorous academic assessment and it turned out that the gaming methodology was equally as impactful as other methods such as in-person workshops.

Another major fast-moving consumer goods (FMCG) brand wanted to find out how its customers felt about buying single-use products (while putting across the message that it was planting more trees than it took to manufacture the product). What it found was that perceptions of using the product varied according to the consumers' ethnicity – a surprising result made possible by the nature of in-game ads.

In all these cases, the businesses were blown away not only by the speed at which they could reach their target audiences via gaming, but also by the response rate, which made the medium far more cost-effective than other methods of advertising or conducting surveys. Some organisations are paying six figures for small sample sizes, in the region of thirty responses. However, through games, they can reach many more for a fraction of the cost and receive almost instant results, in some cases from a hard-to-reach audience.

Our hypothesis on the high engagement rates and response levels is that we are talking to people about issues that matter to them, so they respond. Additionally, we are reaching them on their terms in a non-intrusive way and enabling them to take action on matters that they may feel overwhelmed or helpless over, for example, climate change, the energy crisis, water shortage, body image/self-esteem, etc.

This way of communication and gathering data, especially pertaining to sentiment and what people care about, will only get better over time as the methodology and technology improve. The more the technology develops, the more effective (and cost-effective) player communication will become. Artificial intelligence (AI) and ML will be the next stage in this process (see Chapter 9 for more on the future of gaming and its implications).

Diving deeper

> 'There's so much power and capability to gather data and reach different cohorts or segments of the population, and to help drive people or coordinate communities towards more holistic goals that it's inevitable gaming will evolve in that direction.'
> — Marc Merrill, Co-chairman, Co-founder, Riot Games

Another beauty of using gaming in this way is that surveys can be fine-tuned and optimised as you go along. If you detect a weakness or a gap in your initial responses, you can immediately tweak the questions to rectify it, whereas with other methods you might have to wait weeks or months to get data back before you can review the survey and roll it out again.

This new way of gathering sentiment globally can be used for policy making and other types of decision making, especially when it comes to those which impact people and the planet, for example the environmental, social and governance (ESG) decisions of a business. Some organisations are using this advantage to create business plans that are fed first into executive boards, and then into the rest of the organisation before decisions are made. In this way, they can keep up with changing attitudes and emerging trends and ensure that the decisions they are making are in tune with everyone's wishes and intentions – rather than simply hoping that they have made the right decisions based on gut feeling.

Citizen science

A radical and surprisingly successful use of collecting data via games in recent years has been what is termed 'citizen science', whereby players take part in scientific research. This is particularly appealing to those who enjoy problem-solving, but it also satisfies people who simply want to contribute to scientific knowledge and progress and help to solve real-world problems.

An early example of citizen science came when scientists used *World of Warcraft* to predict what would happen if a virus took over the planet, a scenario which would potentially enhance understanding of human behaviour, even though how we behave virtually varies to how we behave in the real world.[73] The key issue in disease modelling, despite its sophistication, is that the biggest source of uncertainty comes from trying to factor in human behaviour. Interestingly, though, many countries were performing regular surveys to better understand human behaviour, in conjunction with YouGov, and we wonder how the response to Covid could have been enhanced by leveraging the power of games to gather insights.[74] Given that a games-industry-wide initiative Play Apart Together had been activated by the World Health Organization (WHO) and Zynga,[75] could this have been used for further data and insights gathering, and human behaviour modelling? Let's hope we don't have to suffer another pandemic to find out as the world does not have the one advantage games have – to press reset and start again.

Another striking example is a game called *Foldit*:

FOLDIT

Foldit (fold.it) is a game devised by the University of Washington with the aim of finding answers to a problem that even supercomputers couldn't solve.

Proteins only function properly in the body when they are 'folded' into the right shape to allow their amino acid components to participate in biochemical reactions. Folding mistakes seem to be associated with a variety of health problems, ranging from allergies to neurodegenerative disorders, so knowing how a specific protein folds into the right shape is important to understanding disease causes and developing new therapies. The problem is that a newly formed amino acid chain could theoretically twist and fold into millions of possible shapes, and trillions of calculations are needed to model even a small protein.

Launched in 2008, *Foldit* put the challenge to gamers, who would compete individually or in teams to achieve high scores based on the stability of their folded structures, and could share strategies in chat rooms and blogs.[76] As early as 2010, *Foldit*'s creators were able to report in a *Nature* magazine article that its 57,000 players were at least equal to and sometimes better than a computer at folding long chains of amino acids into compact three-dimensional shapes.[77]

The article and subsequent media coverage[78] spurred a huge influx of new players, so that *Foldit* now has around 200,000 registered players – of all ages and from all backgrounds – around the world. Top-scoring players have even been invited to the University of Washington to observe their folding strategies, and the game's creators hope that they will be able to design totally new proteins that don't exist in nature, but may help cure diseases such as HIV as well as solve environmental or energy problems.

With other broad-based public scientific networks searching for signs of intelligent life in the universe, looking for stardust and classifying galaxies by shape, gaming has created a new means of scientific discovery and even a new kind of collective intelligence, exploding the myth of the lone scientist waiting for that 'eureka' moment.

Gaming and dementia

Scientists are also using gaming to further dementia research – a nice coincidence in that gaming itself has been shown to reduce the risk of suffering from dementia.[79] A prime example is the game *Sea Hero Quest*:

SEA HERO QUEST

This game was developed in 2016 by Glitchers, a UK indie, in association with Alzheimer's Research UK, University College London and the University of East Anglia to find out more about one of the primary symptoms of incipient dementia: the loss of spatial navigation skills.

Players have to navigate a boat in the sea after attempting to memorise a chart; and every now and then, they are asked for little bits of information about themselves, such as how old they are, their gender and where they live, as well as about their daily habits. These demographics are linked with their behaviour within the game in terms of what they are remembering and whether they are making the same mistakes again and again.

Over 4 million people have taken part in the game, collectively playing for more than 100 years, thereby providing scientists with data that would have taken traditional dementia research 175 centuries to collect. It is, in fact, the largest study on spatial navigation capabilities ever undertaken.

Initial findings show not only that spatial navigation capabilities begin to decline from the age of nineteen, but also that there are fundamental differences in the special navigation strategies of men and women. Men generally perform better than women, but the gender gap is less in countries with greater gender equality. A country's gross domestic product (GDP) also has a significant bearing on performance, Nordic countries being among the highest performing along with the US, Canada, Australia and New Zealand.

Feedback – the holy grail

'In your life, you are a regular person. You work in a bank or a post office and you have a good life. You might not think you are that interesting, you might think you are little, but in the game, your voice is much stronger, and then you can bring a lot to the agenda. You can influence other people about good stuff that can fix the world.'
— Robert Antokol, Founder and CEO, Playtika

Conventional surveys are typically one-way processes: the respondents rarely find out, directly at least, what the results or effects of their responses are. When we answer survey questions, our voices generally disappear down a black hole. Did anyone actually listen? Did any policies change? Was anything positive achieved as a result?

Because gaming is a two-way communication medium, it is easy to follow up on an initial survey. Even with an anonymous survey, such as the one we did for the UN, it is possible to add a box that the respondent can tick if they wish to be kept in touch with the results. It is then a simple matter to let those who ticked the box know what has been actioned in their country or region. 'Closing the loop' in this way is, for us, the holy grail of the gaming methodology, not only enabling players to have their voices heard, but also feeding back to them the decisions that have been made as a result.

Over thirty-six months, a group from Europe, including Playmob, are tackling the issue of closing the loop on policy decisions on climate action, using gaming. The Games Realising Effective and Affective Transformation (GREAT) project kicked off early 2023 and will release intermittent updates on progress over the years.[80] This is a significant project and undertaking that, if successful, will unlock huge potential for games to close the loop for a variety of decisions within policy making around climate change, and beyond.

According to Alan Gershenfeld, President and Co-founder of E-Line Media:

'Whatever impact issue you're addressing,
when you're empowering players to take on
big challenges, it is essential that the player has
agency and there are continual feedback loops
that their actions are making a difference –
even if they are small. If you accomplish that in
a collective way, sustained over time, you can
make enormous changes.'

In fact, we can go one stage further by asking players what impact those decisions have had on them, so that the process becomes a continuous cycle – a virtuous circle. In this way, gaming can take polling, voting and, indeed, democracy to another level where people feel empowered rather than merely consulted or, worse, ignored.

Games studios already realise the power of engagement with their player base and feeding back to them when changes have been made – by doing so, they should raise engagement to another level. Riot Games, for example, has a Micro Survey Feedback tool that it can deploy within *League of Legends* to target accounts, either randomly or by different criteria, with one or multiple questions to get data back quickly. As Co-chairman and Co-founder Marc Merrill explains, 'We often utilise that to improve the game, but there's a lot of power in the direct-to-consumer relationship not only to learn, but also to direct attention or channel interest.'

Summary

- Gaming is a two-way communication tool that allows players to express their views and be heard on a global scale.

- Its potential to reach vast numbers of people quickly, cheaply and in a highly targeted way, as well as to obtain real-time feedback from them, has been exploited by many organisations, including the UN.

- World-changing action, such as policy changes on climate, can be carried out from valuable in-game data.

- We can view games as a new way to think about platforms for change – for gathering valuable insights from diverse audiences to create social movements.

- Games can be used for scientific research, modelling human behaviours and reactions to scenarios.

- We need to tell players the outcomes of their efforts to speak up on decision making and positive steps forward for the planet. Engage them more in the topic and the game.

6
Playing To Save The Planet

'The big advantage the games industry has is its massive reach, especially to teenagers. They don't really watch TV anymore, but they do play games, so this is a great way to let them take action on issues that matter to us and them, for example the climate.'
   — Ilkka Paananen, CEO and Co-founder, Supercell

The UN SDGs, which stemmed from the Millennium Development Goals, were launched in 2015 with the aim of making the world a better place for everyone by improving education, combating poverty, fostering world peace, developing infrastructure, protecting the oceans and, above all, tackling climate change. The UN set a fifteen-year timeline, which meant that the goals were to be met by 2030 – and we are already over halfway there. Big names such as Film Director Richard Curtis have set out on a mission to 'make the goals famous' and ensure that everyone knows about them, as we cannot change what we don't know needs changing. As we saw in the previous chapter, the gaming industry is committed to the SDGs, and especially SDG 3, 'Good Health and Well-Being', followed by SDG 15, 'Life on Land'.

There are seventeen SDGs. At the bottom, underpinning everything else, are the goals relating to the biosphere – for the simple reason that if we don't have a safe and healthy biosphere, none of the other goals matter. Stockholm Resilience Centre created a pyramid that shows SDGs in a clear and easily accessible format. You can view this on their website.[81]

Earlier in this book, we touched on the question of how games can be good for us – in other words, how they can positively impact our health and wellbeing (see Chapter 4) – and looked at how gaming can be used to enhance education and training (also Chapter 4). In this chapter, and indeed in the book as a whole, we want to focus on the thing that matters most to our interviewees (some of whom are quoted throughout this book): the planet. This is the subject gamers are also most concerned about, as we will see in the next chapter.

It is one of the most pressing issues of our time, no longer something which concerns someone else. We are all starting to feel the impact of climate change on our own doorsteps, through extreme weather and food and water shortages. We are also seeing mass migration and species becoming extinct – disappearing from our planet for good. Almost all sectors and organisations have a strategy on how to protect the planet, to lower their footprint and try to turn back the clock on emissions.

The games sector has a huge opportunity and responsibility not only to be proactive on emissions, but to use gaming as the biggest public service platform to fight climate change head on. Games can be used to raise awareness, take action, drive change and for advocacy. Games can influence individuals, businesses and even governments.

Examples of some activations to date are:

- *PAC-MAN* players were able to play a forest-themed adventure mode with six stages. An album filled with collectibles and a skin (a download which changes the appearance of characters in the game) were the reward for the event completion.

- *Minecraft*, a 3D computer game where players can build anything, added an additional lesson plan on radical recycling to player maps, and as a result was able to make a $100,000 donation to the Nature Conservancy.

- *Pokémon Go* created a first-of-its-kind avatar item to give players a new way to voice their support for sustainability efforts.

- *Angry Birds* fans were able to collect a special mariner hat set for participating in a sea adventure, and the campaign reached over 280,000 people.

- For *Anno 1800*, a city-building real-time strategy video game, PC players would usually grow settlements and create massive production chains in a world with infinite resources. More recently, they've learned how their decisions would affect the environment in the real world and could end up destroying it.

Yet the true potential of gaming has yet to be realised, hence why this book is addressing the opportunity to mobilise the industry to do more, and to mobilise other industries to see games through a new lens and collaborate to tackle the climate crisis. No one organisation or sector can tackle this alone; collaboration is key.

The Playing for the Planet Alliance

'Thanks to a global relevance that spans age groups and demographics, the games industry has a critical role to help raise awareness of the importance of environmental sustainability, help its users start to discuss the issues with their communities offline and spur them to take action.'
— Tamzin Taylor, Head of Google Play Partnerships in Western Europe

The Alliance started as an idea in 2018, after we got to know Sam Barratt from UN Environment and discussed ways in which we could bring the games industry together to take more collective green action. We discussed leveraging the power and scale of the industry to tackle climate issues, but we didn't know quite how yet.

There were sporadic initiatives happening in the games industry already, but we felt if we brought everyone together, we could make an even bigger impact. Some games companies were publicly listed and had to fulfil ESG requirements. Others were under pressure externally from investors or stakeholders or internally from boards or employees wanting them to do more. Some wanted to do more simply because they felt it was the right thing to do. We found other studios had the desire to take action, but were just too small, and therefore time and resource constrained, so had to focus on the day to day rather than having time to think about being green.

Others genuinely created positive planet initiatives for impact and would listen to their players to grow these initiatives. Organisations such as Niantic who, via *Pokémon Go*, started beach clean ups by promoting these to players and rewarding them for taking part in cleaning up the planet. They expanded this to include parks, rivers and other land-based water areas, for those not close to beaches. This was by popular player demand. Other studios have dedicated their games to being pro-planet, such as WildWorks' *Animal Jam* which educates and inspires kids to explore and protect the natural world around them.

The Alliance started with some research on where we were at the time, looking at what games studios were doing already in terms of environmental impact, carbon footprint of the industry, etc. We then talked to people within the industry to see if they would be interested in doing something collaboratively. One of the great things about the games industry is that, although the various studios are in intense competition with each other, it is quite collaborative. Could we get the likes of Xbox and PlayStation to sit next to each other and work together?

Rather than just set something up and hope for the best, we decided we would raise our heads above the parapet with the Playing for the Planet report. The report was written by Trista Patterson, who worked tirelessly to co-found and launch the alliance. Trista is now Chief Sustainability Officer for Xbox.

We launched the report at the Game Developer Conference (GDC) in San Francisco in 2019, where we had dinner with key people from the industry and talked about what we could do. The dinner and discussion opened up ideas like 'let's create this massive game together and get everyone solving problems for climate change in it', but as we all knew, games take a lot of money and time, and we were already running out of time. We also knew we needed something for the industry to own, run with and grow. Plus, not all gamers have the time or attention span to play a detailed game. We needed quick action and ways to engage players via the games they were already playing.

Quite a few ideas came out of that dinner. When we regrouped, we agreed that the best thing for us to do would be to create a group that was member-driven, so that it took ideas from within the industry and worked for everyone. We put this concept to the people who had come to the dinner, and they loved it, suggesting that the group check in together every couple of months to make sure that everything was moving forward as it should.

We also agreed that all members of the group should adhere to two basic rules: they must commit to their studios becoming carbon neutral, if not carbon negative, by a certain date; and they should enable their players to take green 'nudges' by leveraging the power of storytelling and action inherent in the gaming space. Thus the Playing for the Planet Alliance was born.

The Alliance was officially launched at the 2019 UN General Assembly, when its twenty founding members stood up and made their commitments at a UN press conference. Twenty members who were brought together via a roadshow carried out by Lou Fawcett, COO of Playmob. With determination, passion and tenacity, Lou and the team managed to get some of the biggest names in the industry onboard.

Since then, many other studios have joined the Alliance, which today includes forty-nine members, with a collective reach of 1.4 billion monthly players – almost 50% of the players on the planet. The brave and proactive leadership shown by Phil Spencer of Microsoft and Jim Ryan of PlayStation will inspire others, and has done so already, to take action. When true leaders step up to the plate, others follow fast, and we are ever grateful for their belief and action to green the industry with urgency.

The Alliance has four core objectives:

1. To rally the industry to reduce its carbon footprint and to ensure it has the tools to measure, reduce and set targets to decarbonise

2. To inspire environmental action through Green Game Jam activations

3. To share the learnings of initiatives so that others within the industry can follow suit

4. To explore strategies for the future around new games and approaches to storytelling

We will be looking at the Alliance's success in relation to Objective 2 in the next section and to Objective 4 in later chapters. With regard to Objectives 1 and 3, it has created a shared learning environment that has led to action on reducing the industry's footprint.

Clash of Clans creator Supercell led the way in this respect by calculating its overall carbon footprint as a studio and devising a model for other studios to develop. The challenge was taken up by Space Ape, who added factors such as the average amount of energy consumed for a certain amount of playtime, including device charging and leaving a device on standby versus switching it off, plus the energy used by host servers and ad networks, and the impact of live game updates (as opposed to the traditional method of releasing updates periodically).

Once such calculations have been made, of course, there is the question of what studios should do to reduce their carbon footprint. Should they change servers or ad networks, for example, or travel less or in a different way? Should they purchase carbon credits, raise money, plant trees…? Many feel that what we know now is the tip of the iceberg, but there are still a lot of unknowns which the industry needs to uncover, and this can only be done via shared learnings and collaboration.

Here, the Alliance's link with the UN is invaluable, as it gives members access to world experts in reducing and offsetting climate impacts. With the help of the UN and other impact experts, they can be shown how to take small actions that will have big results, such as simply reminding players – after or during a game or even within the game – to power off their devices when they stop playing or unplug their phones once they are charged. We will return to this topic in Chapters 9 and 10.

Below are some of the highlights from the Alliance's key achievements in 2022.

OUTREACH HAS TRIPLED TO 636 MILLION SINCE 2021

 11% OF PLAYERS STATED INTENTION TO CHANGE BEHAVIOUR

 NEW TOOLS AND FRAME-WORKS TO HELP GAMES REDUCE EMISSIONS

 RAISING AWARENESS AT MAJOR GAMING CONFERENCES

 81% OF 400K GAMERS SURVEYED SAID THEY WANT MORE GREEN CONTENT

 REAL-WORLD IMPACT WAS GENERATED WITH 2.5 MILLION TREES PLANTED

 PACKAGING PROTOCOL TACKLED WITH A NEW WORKING GROUP FORMED

 6 NEW MEMBERS JOINED THE ALLIANCE - TOTALLING 49 IN 2023

 NEW SECRETARIAT SET UP TO HELP WITH NEW TOOLS AND RESOURCES

The Playing for the Planet's Annual Impact Report revealed that 2022 was a record-breaking year when it came to rolling out actionable sustainability measures.[82] Thirty+ gaming studios facilitated the planting of more than 2.5 million trees, reached over 600 million players with environmental messaging and encouraged 54% of Alliance members to commit to a decarbonisation ambition.

The success of the Alliance in such a short space of time has caught the attention of many, within and without the climate space. As a model for creating alliances in gaming to support the global goals, it can be replicated to tackle some of the biggest issues being faced in the world – the issues games and the gaming community can work together to resolve. Imagine having a Playing for Education Alliance, Playing for Health and Wellbeing, and so forth. There are endless areas of impact that we can all tackle if we come together for the planet in the way the games industry has done.

The Green Game Jam

'80% of gamers believe climate change is already influencing their lives, 81% would like to see environmental content in-game and 61% would pay for it when it adds to the experience.'
— The Green Game Jam Player Survey 2022[83]

The creation of the Playing for the Planet Alliance revealed that many games companies were taking actions in relation to climate change, but those actions were sporadic and uncoordinated. In bringing those companies together, we were able to combine efforts and impact and really show the world the power of playing for the planet when forces and missions are aligned.

The idea for the Green Game Jam came from John Earner, Co-founder of Space Ape, during a brainstorming session. It was then brought to life by John, Deborah Mensah-Bonsu, Founder of DMB Crew, and Mathias Nørvig, CEO of SYBO Games. The core of the Jam is centred around innovating on existing games with existing audiences for immediate impact rather than creating games from scratch.

The power of existing games is that they already have an audience, so green activations can instantly reach people and make a difference as soon as they are live. All disciplines can participate in the Jam as all roles in a studio can be involved in an activation; some more complex activations may require more people and light-touch activations require fewer. All the participants will come from the same company as they are all usually working on their own existing games, and once an activation has been implemented, they are all expected to go live.

The Green Game Jam is different to a normal game jam – which is where people come together for an accelerated game creation – as the timeframe is over a longer period rather than a few days. The Jam was born during the pandemic, which means it is all about flexibility, working from home and finding effective ways of collaborating without being in the same place. Its window runs from around February to June, and teams decide how best to structure their Jam to submit their concept by the deadline.

Since the Green Game Jam launched in 2020, its value has proved to be inestimable. The impact it's generated has been enormous, from players reached with green messages to trees planted. The latest Green Game Jam survey even noticed a change in behaviour. Having the time carved out to hear from experts and share ideas, studios created a forum to challenge themselves and put forward their best ideas that would have a positive impact on the planet and the game. This forum to share and learn is hugely valuable to keep improving how activations are implemented.

The Green Game Jam has given the industry something to shout about collectively. There is now a panel of judges who select winners within certain categories such as 'UNEP's Choice', 'Media's Choice', 'Most Adoptable' and so forth. The Green Game Jam will not only engage players in environmental issues and enable them to take action, but it will also raise awareness and inform industry stakeholders on the importance of, and interest in, these issues.

Each year, we learn from the Jam before and try to improve it, to increase the number of games in the mix and, above all, to make it more effective. The subsequent Jams have had Lisa Pak, previously of Wooga, to thank as well as Deborah, who is involved to this day.

It is all very well to devise actions and raise money and awareness, but so what? What is it leading to? Once again, we rely on the UN and impact experts to give us that sense of direction.

Part of the process is finding out how players react to the actions taken and the games devised as a result of the Green Game Jam. In 2021, Playmob leveraged its playable ad platform and surveyed players to ask them how they felt about the green activations in-game. Did they enjoy them? Did they want to see more of them?

We then realised that what we should be doing is looking at their attitudes before as well as after that experience, to see whether the Jam had actually managed to move the needle in terms of knowledge, sentiment and behaviour. Had we changed player perceptions of the environment and, more importantly, had they changed the way they played and the way they lived their lives as a result? Also important, had they enjoyed the green game content experience?

The results were then published in the Gr Game Jam Player Survey 2022.[84] We were overwhelmed by the feedback we received. A typical response rate to

Playmob's surveys is 30%, and rich media response rates can be as low as 1%. Not only did 80% of those surveyed respond (some 400,000 people), and in a short space of time, but the level of engagement that we saw was really high – 23% of respondents clicked the external link at the end of the survey, which shows deep engagement as they were taking further action to learn or do more.

Key results of the Green Game Jam Player Survey 2022

Playing for the Planet Alliance Green Game Jam 2022 Player Survey results (344,578 respondents):

- Over three-quarters (78.6%) of gamers believe that 'gaming can help you learn about the environment'.

- Over half (52.9%) of gamers say that environmental issues are already affecting them now, and 26.4% say they will at some point in their lifetime. Only 5.7% say they do not think they will be impacted.

- Nearly half (47.9%) of gamers get their information about environmental issues or climate change via social media. Only 5.3% of gamers do not currently get any information about these issues.

- 35.4% would like to see (or see more) environmental content in their games; 46% want to see it 'frequently'; 13.5% don't want any such content.

- 61.1% are motivated to pay for environmental content if it adds to their game experience, supports a good cause or teaches them something new; 46%

would do so if that content fits within the game's universe or narrative; 13.5% would not.

- 73.4% pledged to take action to change their behaviour.
- There was an 8.8% rise in commitment to action from before playing the green game content to afterwards, with the most popular being going vegan or eating less red meat.

This year (2023), we are planning an even longer-term longitudinal study to find out whether players continue their positive behaviours – and how much for how long – after the game and what they would like to see more of in the future. Once again, the power of gaming as a two-way communication channel enables us to take fast and effective action and really influence human attitudes and behaviours.

Another benefit of the Green Game Jam has been to make it easier for games studios to develop successful green game content. As we will see in Chapter 8, while some studios find it relatively easy to make this happen, others don't even have time to think about it. The Jams have shown us ways of enabling them to overcome the day-to-day challenges that prevent them from engaging fully with green game development, and tools that will help them answer questions such as: how do we make these games engaging and fun? If we are raising money, where should it go? How do we make our actions both effective and credible?

However, there is much more work to be done here. Understanding how environmentally-themed content can interact with our players' attitudes and beliefs will help us be more impactful with future work and get the most out of Green Game Jams. It would be highly beneficial to conduct identical pre- and post-activation surveys and carry out a thorough statistical analysis of the results.

Layering on other data such as game type/genre, audience, activation type, engagement and monetisation metrics will help us understand which green activations are the most effective at increasing awareness and changing environmental attitudes. Targeted thematic questions – for example, those relating to different types of green actions – may be more efficacious than others. Including additional questions around the geography of respondents and their predisposition towards these issues will also be helpful in contextualising results.

Through the Green Game Jam, we look to create best practices for studios to adopt so that they can activate their millions of players around environmental subjects via the games they know and love. We will be looking at player activations in more detail in the next chapter.

While the third Green Game Jam was in progress in the UK, in May–June 2022, the Yale Program on Climate Change Communication and Unity in the US undertook its own nationwide study of gamers' attitudes towards climate change. Its results are summarised in the next chapter.

Platforms for the planet

'What excites me about the power of games is the reach and promise to help players become more aware of the threats to their local environment, what they can do about it and how they can be a voice for change.'
— Tamzin Taylor, Head of Google Play Partnerships in Western Europe

When Playmob started back in 2012, the original concept was to raise money for causes through games as a way to combat global and local issues, while enabling studios to drive deeper engagement and monetise their games. This was inspired through the work Zynga did raising funds for the victims of the Haiti earthquake in 2010, and doing this by engaging players and selling in-app purchases (IAPs) for fundraising. Zynga noticed an uplift in new spenders, existing spenders, lifetime value (LTV) and virality.

Playmob went on to develop a platform and run over fifty activations across the industry, and saw a similar uplift when activations were done well. Ten years on, Playmob subsequently pivoted as the original concept was too early for the industry, and now focuses on data and insights for good.

The opportunity to raise funds for causes through games is enormous, and probably one of the biggest areas of change making in the industry. Within the hit game *Fortnite*, Epic Games raised $50m for humanitarian efforts in Ukraine in three days by donating profits over this short period of time.[85] This is on the same level as some countries' support for aid.

In 2021, Riot Games raised over $7 million for charity with a premium character skin inside *League of Legends*.[86] Players were able to purchase the Elderwood Ornn charity skin between December 2020 and January 2021. The proceeds from all sales were donated to the Riot Games' Social Impact Fund, a venture fund set up by the company to invest in numerous non-profits and games-centric initiatives across the globe. Founded in 2019, the fund is a separate entity from Riot's development and publishing arms. According to the company, the fund has generated over $15 million for various causes. In 2020, the company raised $6 million with a different charity skin, Dawnbringer Karma. Players were also able to nominate non-profits in their local areas to receive a percentage of the funding.

The time is now right for platforms to enter this space, unleash the power of games to do good and appeal to the gamers' philanthropic side, and help studios achieve their impact goals. As we will learn later, studios face many challenges, including pressures on time and resources, and constraints on technology and roadmaps. If tools were developed to mitigate these obstacles, studios could generate even more positive impact.

The focus on protecting the planet has seen platforms such as Games Forest Club emerge. With games and gamers, this platform is protecting forests, while those such as Ecosia and Ecologi which are not developed for games but can be linked to gaming, have been used to enable gamers to plant trees and decarbonise the planet.

However, there is an opportunity for a platform to go bigger and broader to tackle a number of areas in the climate space, and be 'games first'. A platform developed with the needs and constraints of games is essential. It may be a space for popular engines Unity or Unreal to tackle, but it is not core to these businesses. To do this properly requires a team with big ambitions and a focus on gaming, and players such as PlanetPlay could have what it takes to unlock the global player power building up.

PlanetPlay, a non-profit organisation founded in 2021, is supporting games studios to connect to decarbonising projects through IAPs, in-game actions and a marketplace. It is building a platform to take all the heavy lifting away from games studios, from project selection, impact tracking and reporting, to deeper player engagement, all with a games-first approach thinking about both simplicity of integration (a simple application programming interface (API)) and building deeper engagement with the player, for example by offering community features, rewards and money off games and content. Many studios have reviewed the platform and model, and feedback has been along the lines of 'This is what we have been looking for over the past six years of running in-game activations!'

Rhea Loucas, Founder and CEO of PlanetPlay, stated:

'I founded PlanetPlay as a gamer who is deeply concerned about our planet, while recognising the huge potential the games industry has to correct this. To encourage everyone to take actions, we have to ensure the actions are simple and joyful, so we will all repeat them. The games industry's scale, global reach and the speed with which it can engage people are critical for supporting large-scale climate projects, but more importantly, it gives 3 billion people an easy way in to help the world.

'To make this work, it has to be a win-win-win for players, games studios and our planet, so when PlanetPlay was founded, we focused on providing the most simple solution to free games studios from constraints like limited resources, time and knowledge. At the same time, we provide positive uplift for games studios, so everyone can join.'

Despite PlanetPlay being a new player in this space, it has traction and is already seeing results for games studios which align to the early Zynga activation results and the data that was coming out of Playmob activations ten years ago. The only difference is that the engagement and action from players are deeper – the increase of spend and virality is higher, probably due to the awareness of climate action being greater today.

This traction with studios and engagement with players is a positive sign that the industry and gamers want to do more for the planet. Platforms such as PlanetPlay can start to unlock the planet-positive power games possess by taking away the heavy lifting from studios and enabling them to concentrate on making great games.

It is only a matter of time before the engines come into this space, but as we mentioned earlier, it is not core to their business. Many studios like the fact that PlanetPlay is a not for profit, so there could be a great opportunity for the engines such as Unity or Unreal to notice and join forces with PlanetPlay to provide scale to the positive planet actions delivered by the impact platform.

Due to the heavy lifting for activations to happen, they tend to happen infrequently, while many studios are looking for an always-on solution or switch on and off. In later chapters, we discuss the barriers and blockers to unlocking the impact through activations for the industry. We'll then look at some of the ways we can unlock that impact.

Gaming has a huge opportunity to be the hero in this story, to save the world and its people from climate disasters, but we need to work together and create these innovative solutions to enable studios to fulfil their impact potential. We must also understand the world of gaming to create a truly impactful solution which does good for business too.

Apple and Google have made green commitments as organisations, and are working hard on their carbon footprint reduction and eradication. However, there is more they can do and have been doing with their platform power. For instance, merchandising games and apps which are supporting the planet, especially around green moments such as Earth Day and World Environment Day, makes a huge difference to games studios (in terms of discovery) and to players looking to take action for the planet on these special days. Editorial by these platforms also plays a big part in enabling good green games and apps to be discovered.

Convenors have the opportunity and the power to make the impact event greater – which is a win for the platform, the studio, the player and the planet. By choosing to display and promote games that do good, they can amplify the good. Simple decisions such as these can have a huge and long-lasting impact.

Summary

- Games can cover a wide range of impact, but we must focus on the foundations which uphold the rest of the impact we have to make – protecting and preserving the biosphere.

- The Playing for the Planet Alliance was formed in 2019 as a means to combine the efforts of the gaming industry to bring about meaningful change and protect our precious planet.

- It has since contributed to great advances in learning and influence, reaching over 1.4 billion players.

- The Green Game Jam is an annual activity which is built for engaging players in green actions.

- We have so far discovered that the majority of gamers want to take action for the planet while they play and have learned from the activations so much, we are even seeing uplifts in positive behaviour.

- We need platforms to support the heavy lifting of activations, to enable games studios to do what they do best: build great games. The platforms focus on generating the impact.

7
Engaging With Players

'The vast majority of players want to do the right thing, want to do good, but you have to make sure that the [games] companies have actually enabled that to happen.'
— Ilkka Paananen, CEO and Co-founder, Supercell

In the last chapter, we saw how the gaming industry has come together to confront the issue of combating climate change in a concerted and organised way. In this chapter, we will look at the impact studios' actions are having on players (are they engaging with green content?) and on their businesses (does doing good help?).

We have talked about the enormous power of games and their potential for good, but those are of no use if players don't engage with them or enjoy them – if they don't actually care about the planet and how they might help to save it. Is there evidence that gamers want to do good while they play or is all this green gaming just an inconvenience for them? Are they actually buying a product or service because it promises to do good, and by doing so they can make an impact and feel good about themselves?

Surveys such as the Yale Program on Climate Change Communication and Unity, referenced below, have shown that there is a significant proportion of people who simply don't care (not to mention a number who deny that climate change is even happening or that we humans have anything to do with it). There is also an encouraging number who really do care and are doing what they can to make a difference. Inevitably, in between, there is a large body of people who are indifferent or feel that they individually cannot make a measurable impact.

It is largely this last group who are the target of industry actions, since by swaying them away from the 'don't cares' to join the 'do cares', we can turn the needle noticeably in the right direction. Persuading consumers to switch brands – away from ones that don't do good towards ones that do – will also provide an uplift to the industry as a whole and to the most persuasive brands and games in particular.

Doing good while having fun?

'Games give us agency and help us learn new concepts and systems, to try things out and fail and try again. They help us empathize and bring us

so much joy that they provide us with the perfect
platform to take positive action, while having fun.
When we play, we are open to learning, collaborating
and solving problems, let's use these skills towards
the greatest challenges our world faces today.'
  — Deborah Mensah-Bonsu, Founder,
    Games for Good

There has been a rising trend in the past decade of
the more conscious consumer. The 2021 Consumer
Intel Report by Vericast states that 52% of respondents
believe it is important that the brands they purchase
from have values aligning with their own.[87] In addition, 72% of Millennial parents are more likely to be
loyal to a brand or store that shares its efforts to be
environmentally responsible or has sustainable or
ethical business practices. Sustainability is worth a
financial commitment for some – 63% of Millennials
are willing to pay more for sustainable products.

Gamers are no different; in fact, if anything, they
are more aware of climate change issues, more concerned about them and more willing to do something
about them than the average person. In 2017, the
Charities Aid Foundation (CAF) stated that '87% of
gamers think developers are ideally placed to raise
awareness of social/charity issues'.[88] For the great
majority of players, then, it is a win-win situation:
being able to do their bit for the planet while enjoying themselves playing their favourite games, so more
players are engaged in purposeful content. 'I'm doing
something I would have done anyway, and I'm doing
good at the same time.'

Admittedly, some players are content to do good in the background – perhaps to offset their guilt over playing a game for hours – but others are actively engaged. They want to learn more and do more, so they play the game more or look for other games that make an impact. Once they've played the in-game green content, a portion want to do more and go on to take further action.

In their 2021 article reporting the results of an online survey undertaken during the Covid-19 pandemic, Matthew Barr and Alicia Copeland-Stewart drew attention to specific reasons why players are drawn to games with a positive environmental impact:[89]

- They engender responses that relate to a sense of competence and achievement.

- The reward system leads to feelings of productivity and fulfilment.

- Players feel in control in a way they may not in other aspects of their lives.

As a result of their games having a positive environmental impact, studios are seeing players engaging in multiple ways, and there is a virtuous circle effect. If players want it, then the studios will do more of it – until it becomes part of the very fabric of the game. This to us is the ultimate goal, a win-win-win scenario – good for the game, good for the player and, most crucially, good for our planet.

US attitudes

While the third Green Game Jam was in progress in the UK in May and June 2022, the Yale Program on Climate Change Communication and Unity in the US undertook their own nationwide study of gamers' attitudes towards climate change.[90] It is interesting to compare its results with those from the Green Game Jam Player Survey – though it should be noted that the number of respondents to the Yale and Unity survey was smaller in comparison (2,034 vs around 389,000).

The Yale and Unity survey found that 70% of video gamers are 'very' or 'somewhat' worried about global warming (compared with 64% of the US population overall) and 52% would 'definitely' or 'probably' join a campaign, sign a petition, contact government representatives, volunteer time or donate to organisations working to combat global warming. A further 7% were already participating in such a campaign. These figures contrast with those for the US population as a whole, of which only 27% say they would participate in a campaign for climate action, and only about 1% are currently doing so.

About one in five respondents (22%) had seen or heard content related to global warming as part of gaming in the last twelve months, and 13% said they took actions based on that content. The majority of respondents (56%) said that the gaming industry had a responsibility to act on global warming and should do what it could to reduce its own carbon emissions, and 45% felt that the industry should be doing either 'much more' (14%) or 'more' (31%) in this regard.

About half of video gamers were at least 'moderately confident' that the gaming community, working together, could affect what local businesses (52%), corporations (52%), their state government (50%), the federal government (49%) and their local government (48%) do about global warming.

In a commercial perspective, almost half of respondents (49%) said they had rewarded companies that were taking steps to reduce global warming by buying their products one or more times in the past twelve months, while 43% claimed to have 'punished' companies that were opposing steps to reduce global warming by not buying their products one or more times.

Incidentally, Unity is behind a number of games that aim to educate about the impacts of climate change and encourage positive action, including *Ahi Kaa Rangers*, *Gondwana VR*, *Jungle Heroes*, *Samudra* and *Wildeverse*.

Actions speak louder

'With little time left to course-correct the devastating impact of climate change, we need to turn to all solutions which enable action with scale and speed. Gaming is the only way we can mobilise a global community, to act and speak up for what

matters to them. We are only scratching the surface of the possibility yet to be unlocked!'
— Rhea Loucas, Founder and CEO, PlanetPlay

There is little doubt that gamers are supporting green gaming. The question is: how do we encourage more games studios to put activations into a game, to include something that leads to a real-world outcome and has measurable impact?

This can be – and is – achieved in a variety of ways, from light touch at one extreme to deeply integrated at the other. Some studios adopt simple messaging techniques, and others require players to buy items as they play, a percentage of the money going towards a green action such as planting a tree. Others still go the whole way and weave a green story into the game itself by creating new levels, storylines and characters.

A spin-off benefit of this kind of player activation – apart from an increase in both sales and positive climate impacts – is that, having taken a good action within a game, players are more likely to talk about it (eg, on social media) than if they had merely taken part in a standard game. This leads to a virality increase, which can have immeasurable benefits for the industry as well as for the planet.

Games studios are increasingly designing games with climate-related themes, such as *Imagine Earth*, *Terra Nil* and *Endling: Extinction is Forever*, and creating special merchandising moments on key dates, such as Earth Day and World Environment Day. Below are just some examples of green activations that have been prompted within popular entertainment games.

Supercell in Hay Day activation

Within *Hay Day*, Supercell ran an in-game event educating players about the connection between healthy soil, healthy food and healthy people. Along

with a cookbook and educational messaging, Supercell set a community target of filling 150 million truck orders that, when reached, would unlock a donation to train real-life farmers in regenerative farming practices through the Rodale Institute.

Results:

- Goal of 150 million truck orders was surpassed with 165 million.
- Donation was unlocked to train ten real-life farmers in regenerative agriculture practices, translating to nearly 3,000 acres of land being converted.
- An increase in active players.
- A 5% increase in daily active users.
- 2 million+ total impressions on social media.
- 2 million+ digital cookbooks downloaded.

Ustwo in *Monument Valley 2* activation

Brand new chapter, 'The Lost Forest', was added to *Monument Valley 2* to help educate players about the importance of protecting trees – leading to them signing a petition for Play4Forests and declaring a shared interest in forest conservation.

Results:

- Almost 15k petitions signed (goal was 10k).

- *Monument Valley 2* engagement was increased in all areas by three to five times the usual.

- *Monument Valley 1* engagement, such as the number of impressions and downloads, was two times the average.

- *Monument Valley 2* jumped to number 1 in the App Store ranking for puzzles (previously 11).

Niantic across all games activation

Niantic hosts a Community Day each month where all its players are invited to come out and play its games together. Niantic plants a tree for every player who moves (walks) 5km during Community Day, capped at 100,000 for each day.

Results:

- In 2022 alone, players indirectly planted more than 300k trees via the sustainability campaign that Niantic ran.
- Players have attended hundreds of clean-up events each April.
- As a collective, players have explored more than 38 billion kilometres.

SYBO in *Subway Surfers* activation

In 2022, SYBO's *Subway Surfers* launched the second in-game Play2Plant event as part of the Green Game Jam. Play2Plant is also part of SYBO's game world tour. For every player who participated in the event, SYBO planted a tree with a goal of planting 300,000. In the game, players control a character and a hoverboard to collect points, and make the game environment greener by leaving a trail behind them.

Results:

- Increase in impressions compared to previous content update.
- A 13.5% increase in app store impressions/visitors.
- Significant increase in downloads year on year when compared to previous jams.
- A 37.19% increase in Social Media link clicks on posted content.

Flick Games in *Flick Solitaire* activation

Starting in December 2022, Flick Games partnered with PlanetPlay to incorporate climate action into its games. One example is the creation of a dedicated deck in *Flick Solitaire* called 'Winter Wish', featuring artwork by Aliaga Mirguseinov.

Each time a player purchases the deck, $1.50 is donated directly to a PlanetPlay on-ground green project through an API call. Players will be rewarded with points and can use them to make additional purchases on PlanetPlay.com.

Results:

- A 60% rise in IAP item sales in the Apple store.
- 2.5x more IAP item sales in the Google store.
- 3.5x more IAP revenue via the Google store.
- A 2.6% price rise compare to average IAP items.

Ten Square Games in *Fishing Clash* activation

In April 2023, Ten Square Games launched its Teeny Tiny Truth campaign with PlanetPlay, raising funds for a New Zealand-based NGO supporting clean waterways. Players were invited to participate in an in-game event, which on completion would make a donation to Wai Wanaka through PlanetPlay.

Results:

- $20,000 was raised for the NGO.

- In Earth Week, the campaign had a 30% longer session duration compared to other events (non-impact related).

- During Earth Week, *Fishing Clash* had 45% more spend (IAP) during the event compared to other one-week-long events in this year.

Creative Mobile in *Nitro Nation* activation

 PlanetPlay introduced Creative Mobile to luxury electric vehicle company Piëch Automotive, leading to the launch of the first electric vehicle in *Nitro Nation* as a purchasable and playable item with 50% of every purchase donated to Creative Mobile's climate project, Hongera Clean Cookstove.

This initiative is still live as of May 2023, so at the time of writing, the results have not yet been announced.

Winning the game

'We all love to win. Imagine winning the biggest challenge we have ever faced, global warming. Gamers stand a great chance to be heroes in the real world as well as the games they love to play.'
— Amit Khanduja, CEO at Reliance Entertainment

As we saw in the last chapter, the industry is starting to emerge with a conscience and is coming together to take action for our planet. However, the games studios, big and small, have a fundamental concern that cannot be ignored: they are commercial beasts. Key performance indicators (KPIs) on engagement, audience numbers, churn, monetisation, LTV and so forth are front of mind for busy chief finance officers (CFOs), chief marketing officers (CMOs), producers, studio managers, etc. They cannot do anything which does not achieve growth and they cannot afford to do anything that sets them back or could cannibalise revenue.

Project Drawdown stated in its recent framework for the industry publication:[91]

'At the end of the day, all gaming companies will need to transform how they do business to ensure they can thrive in the era of climate change. Companies will need to integrate climate solutions into their internal systems that drive day-to-day decision-making across all parts of the business model.'

Essentially, a games studio will do what it believes will engage its players, keep them coming back and playing, having fun and really enjoying the game. If a studio can do this by weaving in green activations, then it can engage players in the positive planet actions within the game. The question is: can that engagement be monetised? In other words, can new players be attracted by a green approach? Can lapsed players be reactivated? Can existing players be re-orientated? Can new ways of user acquisition be achieved?

This last point is becoming harder and harder with new data rules on platforms emerging, but if going green can attract a new audience and remind existing players to come back, then the game is on to a win-win-win scenario. We are rewriting the traditional user acquisition rules – engaging gamers in taking positive climate action and attracting them with aligned values and goals. Better for the player, better for the game and better for the planet.

From the business point of view, will the new approach align with KPIs and other business goals? It is all very well doing the 'right' thing – and being seen to be doing so – but unless it is also financially right, it will inevitably be canned.

The signs are that the answer to all these questions is a resounding yes. The challenge is that this information is either not known, not shared or hard to find. Over ten years, we have collated data from what we have seen others do/share, such as the Zynga/Haiti example, what we have done ourselves and, more recently, what we have seen from the Green Game Jam participants and PlanetPlay, and the data they are collecting. This data on the benefits to the business of green in-game activations includes:

- **Increase in DAUs (Daily Active Users)**
- **Increase overall in active users**
- **200% uplift in reactivated paying users**
- **Increased positive sentiment**
- **Increased social media interactions**
- **10%+ increase in LTV (Life Time Value)**
- **4% increase in IAP spend**

As you can see from the examples detailed above, green in-game activations realised an uplift on multiple KPIs, but studios may not be forthcoming to share their data. If more studios were aware of the uplift, they would seriously consider green and/or impactful activations in-game as they would see them as a core part of their strategy to deliver and exceed KPIs. We believe it is the responsibility of studios to now share their uplift success and give more studios comfort that this can be not only good for the planet, but an impactful tool in their box to achieve a variety of KPIs.

The issue studios have, though, is many are too busy to implement impact activations. Some studios have managed to put measures in place to ensure they weave it into daily business and do the right thing, while enjoying a business uplift too. As many of the experts we interviewed for this book commented, it is really down to the size of the studio and how much its people are juggling.

Heini Kaihu, Chief Sustainability Officer of Rovio, creators of *Angry Birds*, listed out her main considerations to embed sustainability into the operations of a studio:

- It's essential to start with the culture and values of the organisation. Additionally, ensure that the sustainability strategy is aligned with the overall company strategy and vision.

- Leaders play a pivotal role in this process, as they must set an example and embody sustainable practices in their talk *and* walk.

- Empowering and scaling with employees is arguably the most critical aspect. This can be achieved through engaging and upskilling, showing how employees can move the company and the surrounding world towards a more sustainable future, and gain valuable new skills while doing that.

- Measuring progress here is crucial to track the impact and identify areas for improvement.

The larger the studio, the more it will put into impact and, potentially, it will have a dedicated person or team to drive it. Mid-sized studios may give the responsibility to someone or a group. Publicly listed studios may have pressure from shareholders and a requirement to up their ESG targets, but the smaller studios may just be trying to make ends meet and not have the capacity to think about how the role of doing good can positively impact their games in a number of ways.

As we saw from the Green Game Jam survey results in the last chapter, players are overwhelmingly in favour of green games. We hope that by highlighting player responses plus uplift on KPIs, we will start to convince more studios that doing good is great for business!

Summary

- We are now in the era of the conscious consumer, and this new consumer mindset is transcending into games.

- The Yale/Unity study and the Green Game Jam survey show first-hand the response from players wanting more green game content to take action for the planet.

- Some studios adopt simple messaging techniques, some require players to buy items as they play, with a percentage of the money going towards a green action, while others go the whole way and weave a green story into the game itself.

- We are seeing the desire to do good in games via benefits to the studios such as engagement, LTV and monetisation. This means that doing good in-game can also be good from a business perspective.

- Games studios are increasingly designing games with climate-related themes and creating special merchandising moments on key dates, such as Earth Day and World Environment Day.

- Understanding how roles and objectives can leverage doing good for business and the planet will be an important realisation for today and the future.

PART THREE
GAMING FOR THE FUTURE

'With a potential audience of 5 billion players by 2030, games are poised to become one of the most impactful forms of entertainment and a powerful vehicle to raise awareness of global issues, like the fight against climate change. It is essential we as an industry play our part to continue reducing our environmental footprint while also encouraging our communities to act and lead the change.'
— Yves Guillemot, CEO, Ubisoft

Given the diversification of games, audiences and player motivations, the potential to deliver powerful messaging and nudge behaviours is immense. Games can now, for example, reach remote parts of Africa via the Internet of Elephants,[92] where people can be educated on the importance of protecting wild animals – how this is beneficial in economic as well as ecological terms. In such ways, games can make lasting changes to people's lives and the planet – changes that, as we saw in Chapter 7, the great majority of players want to happen.

As Chapter 6 showed, the games industry is coming together to optimise its efforts to bring about such changes, but how can it influence other business sectors, non-profits and policymakers to leverage passionate and engaged global gaming communities to create a better real world? How can the power of games to engage and motivate be harnessed by the movers and shakers of the world so that it is used in the best way for our future? Is it utopian to imagine governments, gamers and industry coming together to protect and preserve the planet, through the games we love and play every day?

We attempt to answer these questions in this final part of the book, which shows what progress is already being made in this direction, as well as what remains to be done. We'll includes a unique 'Good Gaming Guide' for gamers, policymakers and the game industry – a roadmap for us all to follow as we make our way forward towards a better world.

8

Doing Well By Doing Good

'The idea of a game as a service where the virtual loops integrate with real-world loops is a huge opportunity. What we're missing is an ongoing feedback loop in the real world. There are big, complicated challenges out there and you need a constant set of feedback loops. If you get that, and get it in a collective way, you can make enormous change.'
  — Alan Gershenfeld, President and Co-founder, E-Line Media

In Part One of this book, we looked at the gaming landscape – who is playing, where and how, and how gaming has changed over the past few decades and is continuing to change today. In Part Two, we considered how games could and are being used for good. We also addressed some of the issues around safety and security that have affected gaming.

We have seen that gaming is a massive and powerful medium that can change mindsets and behaviours, teach and train, and has enormous potential to improve the world. The question is: how can that potential be realised? How can we get gamers, the industry, other business sectors, influencers and policymakers to realise the power at their fingertips and use it as a force for good?

In this chapter, we are concerned with the challenges faced by the games industry, both internally in terms of meeting goals and targets, and externally in terms of collaborating with other businesses and non-profits to activate impactful initiatives, while ensuring the art form of gaming is respected and genuine. As we have seen, there is a large appetite to do more, to work more into existing games to create games for good, but there are still challenges and blockers, especially around the way the industry works, the way roles are assigned and how individuals view their responsibilities and priorities. There are issues of resourcing, time, education and understanding. How can these obstacles be overcome?

There is also the question of technology and how that can enable us to do more good without taking the magic out of the industry. Games are first and foremost about having fun, and we don't want to distract games studios and developers from that priority, to make doing good a burden that takes away from the very reason why we want to play.

Face the challenges

> 'We must remember that the manager's first mission
> is to make the business better, not to change the
> world, yet it's important to be a good human being
> and to think about the world. Because we don't
> have another world. It's hard because at the end of
> the day, we're a public company. We need to focus
> on our revenues, we need to beat our numbers. We
> always need to find the right formula in between.'
> — Robert Antokol, Founder and CEO, Playtika

As we have discovered, the games industry poses a tremendous opportunity to tackle some of the world's greatest problems, including climate change. However, it is not straightforward for studios to run activations. Although many are doing this and more, and doing it frequently, there still remains a blocker to making these initiatives a de facto part of gaming. This is a challenge we remain determined to crack, to unlock the potential for humanity and the opportunity for a positive impact on a studio's bottom line.

For Marc Merrill:

> 'It's a no-brainer to allocate some percentage
> of time, resources and effort to the broader
> general good – not only for individuals in
> the communities, but for the industry, even
> from a self-interested perspective. Studios
> can clearly afford to do that, but it's a long-
> term investment and it requires organisations
> to focus on higher values. If they're publicly

traded, there's often pressure from quarterly earnings targets and the whole focus on profits, which can derail them from those things. They need not only conviction and understanding, but also the capability to appropriately manage the different interests.'

As Rob Small, President and Co-founder of Miniclip, highlighted, 'It depends on the size of the studio. Smaller ones are fighting for survival, whereas larger ones have got the resource and capacity to do more'.

Jennifer Estaris, Game Director, ustwo Games, stated:

'For us in the… "non-serious" side of game development, it's no walk in the park either. Due to tight schedules, engagement goals and limiting constraints, sometimes meaning and social impact can get deprioritised. It has happened to me, but we should keep trying, as these efforts increase game quality and appeal.'

'Consider questions like: how will my game touch someone's heart? How will my game allow people to reflect deeply on our connection with the world and with each other? How can my game catalyse humans to change the world for the better?

These are economic questions. Economy comes from the Ancient Greek *oikos* (household) and *nemein* (manage).

How are we managing our home – Earth – and the family who lives in it – humanity?'

Jennifer Estaris, Game Director, ustwo Games

Doing good vs doing well

As Jennifer Estaris points out, building a deeper connection with players is an economic consideration. If you want your game to do well, consider what they care about. Chances are, many will care about climate change and/or positive impacts they can have on people and the planet.

As we discovered in the previous chapter, games studios are like any other businesses: they are under pressure to survive, succeed and prosper. The time, money and resources they have available for non-key activities are limited, and doing good is often seen as such an activity. Some studios don't feel able to even think about such things; they are focused on making their games as attractive and lucrative as possible, which means keeping their players happy and engaged (by constantly updating and improving their games) so that they keep playing and buying. Showing that weaving planet-positive impact into the ways they engage their players could help them understand that combining these activities could have transformational results.

Other companies may have a requirement to do something – and be seen to be doing something – for the planet. Especially publicly listed companies whose shareholders are striving to achieve ESG goals.

Internally, it is a question of making a business case for doing good in games, which needs to be relevant, interesting and exciting, rather than a fluffy nice-to-have, for the studio as well as for the player. If the CFO can be shown that putting this piece of content in this game will make it appeal to existing customers or, better still, first-time spenders, or attract new players and potential spenders, and therefore improve sales or stimulate more in-game sales or extend playing times, they will get behind it. In free to play, getting a user to pay for anything is difficult, especially for the first time. It has been estimated that getting a mobile gamer to make a first in-game purchase costs an average of over $35.[93]

A CMO may be more interested in the organic growth of their audience base, exposure and ways to drive new players and engage with those who have fallen away from the game. If an impactful activation can get a game more awareness and larger audiences, the CMO would be interested, this being an additional tool in their marketing box.

Putting together a convincing business case to integrate an impact initiative into a game is one of the hurdles to generating more impact through games. This book exists to address this issue, to show that integrating good into games can generate a business uplift, if done properly and genuinely. The previous chapter highlighted uplift data when discussing how players perceive doing good in-game. Through our own research, we saw more players spending money for the first time, players who had fallen away re-engaging, deepening engagement of existing players and boosting virality and social interactions. The key now is to make more studios aware of this uplift and to encourage others to share case studies and data across the industry to prove that by doing good, they are doing well.

Sustainability as a responsibility

'At the end of the day, any business in the games industry is going to thrive on the basis of the talent that it can retain. Let's be honest, talent is everything.'
— Rob Small, President and Co-founder, Miniclip

When it comes to considering how they can do more around social issues or the environment or gaming for good, studios often pass the question to someone in operations or communications or human resources – perhaps someone who is passionate about these topics or perhaps someone who has little knowledge or expertise in that area, and no time to deal with it either. To be fair, many studios are starting to hire specific personnel to take on this role, but even some of the bigger ones are still treating it as a part-time duty – a kind of add-on to an existing role, which inevitably results in the person in that role being overstretched and leaving it to last, especially if they are faced with a steep learning curve.

The Playing for the Planet Alliance (see Chapter 6) was formed with the aim of addressing this problem, among others, and can prevent individual studios having to reinvent the wheel by passing on information, guidelines and even ready-made solutions. We saw in Chapter 6 how Supercell and Space Ape developed a model for calculating a game's carbon footprint, which is now available to all Alliance members to use and build on, and keep adding to over time as new knowledge and expertise emerge.

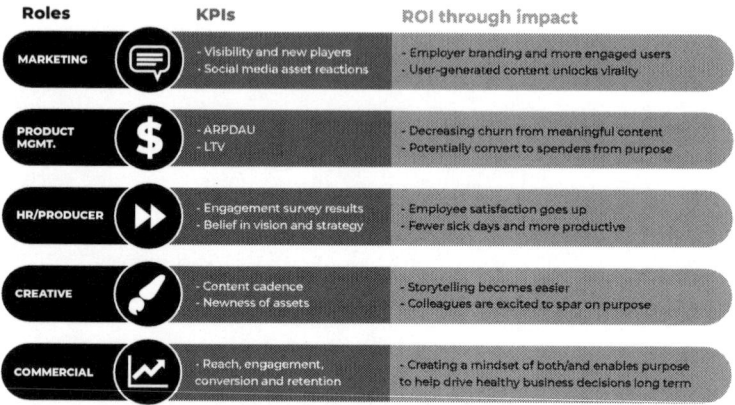

Roles	KPIs	ROI through impact
MARKETING	- Visibility and new players - Social media asset reactions	- Employer branding and more engaged users - User-generated content unlocks virality
PRODUCT MGMT.	- ARPDAU - LTV	- Decreasing churn from meaningful content - Potentially convert to spenders from purpose
HR/PRODUCER	- Engagement survey results - Belief in vision and strategy	- Employee satisfaction goes up - Fewer sick days and more productive
CREATIVE	- Content cadence - Newness of assets	- Storytelling becomes easier - Colleagues are excited to spar on purpose
COMMERCIAL	- Reach, engagement, conversion and retention	- Creating a mindset of both/and enables purpose to help drive healthy business decisions long term

Roles, KPIs and return on investment (ROI)

The person tasked with 'greening' the studio's game is often the one who is most passionate about it, so they end up doing it in their spare time. If they are given free rein to make decisions and get things done, as is sometimes the case, things can happen quickly, whereas if the business structure is such that they have to go to a line manager and then the board to get any sort of approval, the whole initiative can grind to a halt before it has even got off the ground.

As Sir Ian Livingstone, Co-founder, Hiro Capital, states:

'Games makers need to go further to make sure games have a really positive impact on our society. It [gaming] is a social, cultural and economic phenomenon that is often unrecognised at best and sometimes criticised. Yet it has the power to bring people together in multiple ways, and as an industry we need to take full responsibility for that superpower.'

The CEO of Ten Square Games decided to make Olga Ostrowska his sustainability person. She's also involved in operations, so she understands the importance of sustainability being an integral part of running a business. This move has enabled Olga to take ownership on decision making. Because she has not been held back by having to talk to and get approval from layers of management, she has been able to quickly get things off the ground and make an impact. She knows who to bring in when, and how to coordinate the team internally to make decisions, which are operational team decisions and not top-down management decisions.

The Project Drawdown Framework for the Games Industry is set out for employees on sustainability teams who are generally looking to take climate action at work. The suggestions cover:

- Ways to integrate climate action into your and your team's roles

- Evaluating your company's climate goals and identifying areas for improvement

- Communicating to leadership ideas for climate action and real-life examples of success

- If you're in a leadership role, how to formulate long-term strategies for your team and company[94]

Drawdown provides a useful plan in its Job Function Action Guides, which can be leveraged in gaming to help people in various roles understand how they too can weave in positive climate actions at work.[95] Certain areas are outlined as key leverage points for organisations in the gaming industry to align their business with drawdown, which is the future point in time when the levels of greenhouse gases in the atmosphere stop climbing and start to steadily decline. Each area listed below enables a gaming company to take high-impact actions which will help to achieve drawdown quickly, safely and equitably:

- Emissions reduction

- Climate disclosure

- Gamer and community engagement

- Climate policy advocacy

- Products, partnerships and procurement

- Business model transformation

- Investment and financing

- Long-term thinking

For more details on the Project Drawdown Framework for the Games Industry, the full publication can be downloaded.[96]

The aim to achieve drawdown, of course, makes it vital for studios to hire the right people – people who genuinely want to make a difference and have the skills and competence to put their ideas into practice. It is also worth saying that more and more people are inclined to work for companies that have a strong ESG agenda, which means that having a clear message around greening games – and showing that it is being done genuinely and not merely in a 'greenwashy' way – can help the games industry to attract and keep good talent.

Rob Small recognises that people choose to apply to work for a studio because it has a reputation for doing good, and this is crucial today when studios are all vying for the best talent. Showing you care about your people and the planet will go a long way to attracting and retaining the best talent.

Rule 101: Keep players happy

> 'It's a delicate balance. Some people come into games as a form of escapism; they want to get away from the horrors of the real world, and we have to respect that.'
> — Rob Small, President and Co-founder, Miniclip

Showing you genuinely care is something to be mindful of on the players' side as well, because players see right through anything that is not genuine and will kick back on it. It is therefore vital for studios to think about the impact they want to make and how they are going to deliver it in a way that is genuine, cohesive and long-term, rather than just being a one-off box-ticking exercise or a marketing stunt.

Players can be a challenge in other ways, too. We saw in Chapter 7 that the majority of them are fully aware of climate change and other environmental issues and want to do their bit to combat them, but the sad fact remains that a lot of people, gamers included, are not – or even resolutely refuse to accept that there is a crisis and a need for action. One studio spokesperson we talked with mentioned that a good majority of their players were 'climate deniers' and their particular challenge was to 'convert' some of these people to at least some awareness of the issues at stake – without necessarily asking or inviting them to actually do anything about it. The studio did this by turning the global climate conversation into a local one about people who are running out of water or facing extreme weather conditions, and making those people within the game decide how to deal with those problems.

As John Hanke, CEO of Niantic, puts it: 'We need to get people that aren't yet motivated, and then introduce those [climate, environmental, etc] ideas by drawing them into something that seems like it would be a fun experience, and hopefully is a fun experience, first and foremost.' Essentially, it is a matter of adapting games to the audience and framing the topic in a way that will engage them, educate them and, perhaps eventually, move them towards doing something.

There are language challenges, too. As online connectivity continues to grow, localised content, ie, specific language versions of a game, has become one of the biggest barriers to access in non-English speaking markets.

As the makers of some of the world's highest revenue-generating games (including *Fortnite*, *League of Legends* and *Pokémon GO*) have found, engagement leads to revenue. The more engaged with a game players are, the more they are willing to spend. Therefore engagement is a key metric to watch. Where are players hearing about the game? Why do they join? How long do they play in each session and overall? Do they share the game on channels outside of the game and attract others to play? By doing this, games studios can be confident they can monetise through in-game items or/and advertising. By integrating impact into games actions, results can be exceeded because players see that the game cares, and is working towards real world impact they care about.

Giving games impact

'Games are a great way to educate people on important issues throughout the world.'
— Matt Fischer, Apple's Vice President of the App Store

It is, of course, one thing to create a game specifically around a particular topic and quite another to integrate an impactful activation into an existing game. It is always hard to generate a large audience for a new game, in the short term at least, whereas an existing game already has an audience, which makes it potentially far more powerful.

The challenge is to weave the required content into those games without diluting or damaging them and consequently turning players off. Each game is different, and audiences will vary depending on who they are and their tastes, so you need to think through doing something in-game carefully. There are various ways in which integrations can be achieved.

A game being developed from scratch will have planet-positive impact built into the design process, but if it is an in-game integration to an existing game, the type of integration could range from light touch to more involved, the latter requiring more time to fit into the roadmap. Many game roadmaps are locked at least six months ahead, so you need to plan and develop ideas in time. Of course, the type of integration will also depend on the reasons why players play the game, and so knowing the audience is key to having successful sustainable in-game activations.

The image below sums up some of the reasons why players play, which gives an indication of the type of activation they are likely to enjoy. The more they enjoy the game, the more uplift it will see, which as we discussed earlier is key to building a business case internally and enabling activations to happen.

ULTIMATE GAMER

ALL-ROUND ENTHUSIAST

CLOUD GAMER

CONVENTIONAL PLAYER

HARDWARE ENTHUSIAST

POPCORN GAMER

BACKSEAT VIEWER

THE TIME FILLER

Equal representation

While we're striving for a positive impact, it is important to avoid potentially negative impacts. Like other media, games tell stories that convey specific messages about who and what matters. If we want to bring about a global change, it is important that all players, especially children and young people, see diverse, intersectional representations of characters in games that reflect the general population – in terms of race, gender, sexual orientation, ability/disability, etc – and avoid instilling unconscious bias in them.

The Geena Davis Institute on Gender in the Media has found extensive bias in the film industry, for example.[97] Its research concludes that, whereas people of colour constitute 38% of the US population, only 30% of family films feature a lead of colour. Similarly, while 4.5% of people identify as LGBTQIA+ in the US, family films with an LGBTQIA+ lead average less than 1%; and 18.7% of people have a physical or cognitive disability, but only about 1% of the leads in family films are from this group.

Games are in a strong position to re-balance these biases – and many studios are actively doing so. For its game *Beyond Blue*, for example, E-Line Media worked with an impact funder specifically interested in highlighting amazing real-world female marine scientists and explorers. Elsewhere, players of *The Sims* were able to take part in Black Lives Matter rallies (which also enabled the immunocompromised and those with disabilities to participate), evidencing that gaming can not only inspire change, but also empower people to take action, as we discussed earlier.

Beyond the content of the games themselves, the industry is encouraging game development via 'underserved' creators. *League of Legends* developers Riot Games, for example, recently put $10 million into funding such founders and creators to supply more content for underserved groups of players.[98]

Partnerships

'Our first principle is do something that matters.
That means something that's going to impact a large
number of people, even if it's a very small nudge – a
very small change of behaviour that, multiplied by a
billion, has a really large impact.'
— John Hanke, CEO, Niantic

If the industry is to widen and increase the impact of
its green initiatives, it is essential that it forges partnerships with external organisations that are equally
passionate about making such an impact. As we have
seen, the potential for the games industry to lead
efforts to raise environmental awareness and prompt
action is huge.

One of the most effective ways of achieving this
is through partnerships. Playmob's survey of games
studios revealed that collaborations are seen as a
prime way to garner attention for important causes,
showing the power of bringing together public and
private sector organisations.

Actually creating such partnerships is, however,
no easy matter. The games business today is complex and dynamic, with a wide range of platforms
and diverse genres, as well as ever-changing business models and publishing strategies, so finding an
organic alignment between game design, commercial
viability and impact objective, as well as partners that
have a shared risk tolerance and a clearly defined
process of decision making (playing to each partner's
strengths) and conflict resolution, is a major challenge.

However, it can be done and, when done well, can be hugely successful and impactful.

Alan Gershenfeld, President and Co-founder of E-Line Media, begins the process by ensuring stakeholders are aligned around impact objectives, financial objectives and risk tolerance. For example, E-Line was approached by the Cook Inlet Tribal Council, a pioneering Alaska Native organisation, who wanted to make an impact investment in a video game that authentically represented their culture (which has been largely misrepresented in popular media) and could engage a global audience.

Together, they developed an 'inclusive development' process with over thirty Alaska Native elders, writers and storytellers. The resulting game, *Never Alone*, is in the Inupiaq language (and subtitled in sixteen languages). Based on a story passed down thousands of years, it has reached over 12 million players, won a BAFTA and Peabody, and is featured in the Museum of Modern Art and Smithsonian.

As mentioned earlier, E-Line used a similar inclusive development process with marine scientists in its game *Beyond Blue*, and with teachers and learning scientists in youth game-making projects such as *Gamestar Mechanic* (partnership with Institute of Play) and *MinecraftEdu* (partnership with Teacher Gaming). This has empowered millions of young people to become creators, not just consumers of games.

The Sims 4 team has worked closely with the It Gets Better Project and GLAAD to understand the use and impact of pronouns and where binary representations of gender are present in the game. This ensures EA games and experiences better reflect the diversity of the world. Apple, too, has created innovative partnerships with (RED) and the World Wildlife Fund, as well as undertaking collaborative initiatives through its gaming subscription service, Apple Arcade.

Effective partnerships can be with a commercial brand (such as cars for a racing game) or film company (eg, for an action game), or they can be personal (with a musician or a sports celebrity, for example) – anything that will create buzz around a game to attract new players and bring back old ones. The potential for real-world sports fans and gaming sports fans to come together for global good represents an especially large opportunity to harness shared passions and drive change.

Miniclip recruited Joey Kramer, the drummer from Aerosmith, for its *Ultimate Golf* game. Players could play golf against him and money was given to charity. As Rob Small recalls, 'It was a lot of work logistically and it was just a one-off campaign. It did OK, but making these initiatives scalable is the difficult part.' However, where there are challenges around initiatives that pose a potentially huge uplift, there is an opportunity to find solutions and platforms that can align partners and make a match not only work as a one off, but become a sustainable initiative.

Although working with a celebrity or a sports influencer who has a massive following can generate a halo effect, as ever, it is important that the association is authentic. This is where platforms such as

PlanetPlay can support the industry in making genuine and authentic connections. One area it is building is a list of IP, such as musicians, sports celebrities and brands who are all passionate about the planet. With these connections, PlanetPlay is then identifying the right fit in terms of game type and audience, to ensure an enjoyable player experience which makes sense for all and, more importantly, is a genuine effort to make a positive impact on the planet. PlanetPlay launched its first collaboration with Creative Mobile's *Nitro Nation* and electric car brand Piëch on Earth Day 2023. The results at time of writing are yet to be identified.

Working with non-profits

When a games company decides to do something for the environment or to build a game about environmental impact, it often needs to seek advice from organisations with the relevant specialist knowledge. This is the perfect opportunity to create a partnership with a non-profit, as the creators of *Hellblade* did.

Hellblade is a game that teaches players about a mental health condition called psychosis – a psychiatric disorder that leads to distorted reality, hallucinations and delusions – by enabling them to experience similar symptoms. The game's creators, a team of around twenty developers led by Tameem Antoniades, worked with the Wellcome Trust, a London-based charitable foundation focused on health research. The trust actually put some money behind the game

DOING WELL BY DOING GOOD

and supplied expertise by allowing the studio to talk to people who were living with the condition, and neuroscientists and therapists who were treating it. This made sure that the game was realistic, while the games team brought the necessary fun and adventure to it. It was so successful that it scooped up BAFTA awards for everything from visuals to content.

Similar partnerships have been forged by other companies, including WildWorks, which has created games for kids around protecting wildlife and the environment. We are seeing more studios pop up that are building games specifically to teach players something in an entertaining way, such as Lumi Interactive building *Kinder World*, which focuses on mental health and the environment, or Super Authenti, founded by successful game makers and entrepreneurs, which launches in 2024 with *Catly*, a hyper-realistic virtual reality of real-world cats in a nature-oriented habitat. This allows gamers to unveil a never-before-seen nature-verse.

In the game, you can explore and interact with different cat species, learn about their habitats and understand the impacts of climate change. It has stunning visual representations of nature and wildlife to immerse gamers in a world that blends fantasy with reality, encouraging them to think and care about environmental challenges and conservation efforts. *Petaverse* makes it easier for social interaction by allowing players to breed their virtual cats with others, fostering a sense of community within the game.

There are also learning elements about empathy and a sense of responsibility for nature through interactions with virtual creatures, motivating gamers to do comparable activities in the real world. *Petaverse* could shape the future of gaming by inspiring environmental awareness and conservation through an immersive and impactful experience, generating real-world impact in multiple ways, but mainly through connecting with non-profits that are inspiring positive behaviour towards our planet and every living thing on it.

This is a growing trend – entertainment games being built with planet-positive impact and/or educational messages in them, or studios retrofitting this type of content into their games. Games created specifically with learning at their core, as Sir Ian Livingstone highlighted, must be built by those who understand game design and lead with fun first or people won't play and the games will flop.

A good example of this is ustwo in *Alba: A Wildlife Adventure*, a game that offers players 'a sense of freedom and childlike wonder, while also sharing a message that when it comes to protecting the environment, even small actions can have a big impact'. ustwo also partnered with Ecologi to plant one tree for each game downloaded. Another example is Broken Rules' *Gibbon: Beyond the Trees*, an ecological adventure about freedom and survival, which was made with guidance from various NGOs including the Gibbon Rehabilitation Project and Gibbon Conservation Society.

As Apple's Vice President of the App Store, Matt Fischer, recalls: 'What began as a simple adventure game around the movement of gibbons developed into more serious themes as the creators delved deeper into research and learned about the threats facing these small apes today.'

For every success, however, there are games that never reach the shelves because the developers run out of money or into technical troubles, or because the games aren't effectively marketed or distributed or simply aren't fun to play. Especially for an educational and impact-focused game, if it isn't fun, it is doomed. Plus to date, there has not been enough investment or funding available for this category of game.

This shows that it is vital for games studios to think carefully about how they can add impact to games and to apply as much rigour to these games' development as there is in the underlying pedagogical research. Fail to do this, and the growing enthusiasm (and funding) for research-based games could rapidly evaporate and the enormous potential to engage, educate and empower will be lost.

However, things are starting to change. Many games founders who exit and cash out their businesses are looking at how they can apply their skills, networks and resources to gaming for good, so these issues will diminish over time.

This type of collaboration, in addition to the growing body of research on how digital entertainment can transform learning (see Chapter 4), has led to an increasing interest among foundations, universities, government agencies, social entrepreneurs and philanthropists in making video games that have the potential to make a social, educational or health impact. Alan Gershenfeld calls these organisations 'accidental publishers' – non-gaming organisations who have stepped into funding game development with little to no experience in that field.

On the flip side, Rob Small emphasises the importance of educating non-profits as to the advantages of building sustainable relationships with an industry as powerful and valuable as the games industry.

'By giving them our time and our experience and our contacts, we can help them to build internal initiatives that will ultimately allow them to leverage more from the games industry. Initially, we thought, "They just want our cash", but actually that's definitely not the case. They really do want to get inside our heads and understand how they can build more scalable, more sustainable relationships with the games industry, and it's been fun to be involved in that.'

Oliver Miao, Co-founder and Executive Advisor of Pixelberry, also has experience of working with non-profits, including the Cybersmile Foundation, an international non-profit organisation committed to tackling all forms of cyberbullying and digital abuse, and the National Eating Disorder Association. Both partnerships were highly successful; indeed, Miao comments: 'The National Eating Disorder Association didn't realise how powerful games could be.' The Cybersmile Foundation partnership raised hundreds of thousands of dollars for the charity, enabling a helpline to open up twenty-four hours and supporting thousands of people impacted by bullying, especially cyberbullying.

Technology for the world

'Every good business needs to give back to the world, to the community, to the people.'
— Robert Antokol, Founder and CEO, Playtika

Playmob's 2019 assessment of the games industry, which looked at the impact it was making in the areas of health and wellbeing, education and climate change, revealed the importance of bringing together all STEM concepts to form an interactive medium enabling gamers to actively learn new skills and solve problems in unique situations. It is obviously in the industry's own interests to look after the billions of people who play games (as well as to attract more people into the technology sector in general and gaming in particular so that the industry can continue to strive), but it is equally important to look after the wellbeing of people.

Gaming has led the way in so much in technology, being years ahead of thinking and testing approaches, while other sectors typically take on the learnings and apply games and gamification their own way, years later. The growing interest in games making a positive impact is starting to make its way into these other sectors, which are adopting gamified approaches to engage people or leveraging gaming to tap into massive audiences. We have seen this from Playmob's example of working with the UN to collect data for policy change, and from working with the water and utilities sector to leverage gaming to raise awareness of water shortages and sustainable energy solutions.

Summary

- Studios are finding ways to overcome the challenges to doing good through games by weaving the good element into roles and responsibilities.

- Doing good is as much about economic outcomes as ecology. We are learning that doing good in-game translates to doing well for business, and soon there may be an opportunity cost to not doing good!

- The Drawdown Framework is an important one for studios to follow in terms of what to focus on as an organisation and within different roles.

- Keeping players happy is the factor of utmost importance to the games studio, so it's essential to learn what makes them tick and align company values for the best outcomes.

- Partnerships are key to achieving great results –
  working with non-profits, brands and IP.
  A collaborative approach based on the same
  goals will become a sum greater than its parts.

- Making sure activations are equal and inclusive
  is crucial. Think about different perspectives and
  talk to players to ensure equal representation and
  enjoyability for all.

9
Changing The World

'Building awareness is always a great thing, but when you can do something that feels natural and organic to the game and actually influences change, that's where it makes the biggest difference. The games industry is a bullhorn that can amplify things and really affect change among our players.'
— Oliver Miao, Executive Advisor, Pixelberry

Given its vast and ever-increasing popularity and its power to engage and influence, gaming is now a cultural megatrend and phenomenon which touches our lives in so many ways, whether we realise it or not. How can we ensure that it will drive its culture in the right direction and lead to change in the real world?

In this chapter, we look at ways in which we might achieve this while respecting the art form that is gaming, ways it has worked in the past and – an essential ingredient to unlocking the impact potential of the industry – the leadership it requires to enable games and gamers to become real-world heroes. Without the right type of leadership, our true power of play could be lost or, worse, take us down a different path.

When given the choice, choose right

'Small steps is a good place to start. We're not going to solve this overnight, so let's just get on the road. Whether it's recycling, whether it's changing our electricity provider for our office, we've all got to get on that journey and start making those steps.'
— Rob Small, President and Co-founder, Miniclip

The first thing to be clear on is that gaming isn't going to solve all the planet's problems overnight. All of us – the industry, stakeholders and gamers themselves – need to be realistic and keep in mind that it is a gradual process, which starts with awareness of the issues and problems, and then motivates and enables people to do something about them, however small. What games companies are trying to do is not be the whole solution, but be that starting point of enabling people to do something small while seeing the bigger impact, to understand that they can go on to do more – whether it be tree planting or switching from driving all the time to taking public transport. It is about nudging people and starting to change their behaviour. Our days are full of decisions, so when given a choice, if we choose right, we will make progress in the right direction.

In Chapter 6, we saw the importance of the Playing for the Planet Alliance's link with the UN in reinforcing this message within the industry. We know that games are a powerful medium for initiating changes in mindset and behaviour. Rather than being a purely passive experience, such as watching a film, gaming makes the player part of the story, in which they must not only understand, but also tackle the issues at stake. Through the game, they become activists.

In her talk at the 2023 Pocket Gamer Connects, a leading international conference series for the global games industry, ustwo Game Director Jennifer Estaris emphasised how small numbers can inspire change and drew a parallel with non-violent protests.[99] While they may not draw massive participation, almost all non-violent protests have achieved their goals of reaching a participation threshold of just 3.5% of the given population. This research is from Harvard's Carr Centre for Human Rights Policy, and naturally there are exceptions to this rule.[100] However, it's a useful benchmark – in the UK, that's only 2.3 million people.

For game developers, that's achievable, so what can they do to help spread a positive influence? As we have seen, games are played by almost 50% of the world's population, so 'playtivism' (a term championed by Estaris) has an immense and unprecedented potential to inspire change. *Mission 1.5* proved that we can leverage games to impact policy making. The reach is there and the speed to ask players questions is almost instantaneous – in just three weeks, a 56% representative sample of the global population was reached.

The only thing stopping us achieving 100% is access to technology – devices and the internet, but that will come. One of the most powerful things games studios can do is leverage their player base to speak up on what matters to them, and get this information to policy makers and CEOs, putting pressure on major decision makers to act quickly now, and in the right direction.

As we saw in the previous chapter, John Hanke, CEO of Niantic, underlines the importance of making a difference, however small:

> 'Our first principle is do something that matters. That means something that's going to actually impact a large number of people, even if it's a very small nudge, a very small change of behaviour that, multiplied by a billion, has a really large impact.'

If we all implement the right thing in our daily lives, in the games we design and the teams we manage, the games we play at home and how we play them, our small actions can generate a huge impact. Especially for the games industry and the gaming community.

Growing the impact

'It's a big world, so we all have to ask ourselves, how can we leverage the power that we have – the company, the resources, the user base, the product design – to have the maximum impact?'
— John Hanke, CEO, Niantic

An increasing number of studios are developing games with environmental themes and challenges, which serve to inform as well as entertain. Examples are Sam Alfred's *Terra Nil*, in which players 'undo' environmental degradation using technologies such as a toxin scrubber; Ubisoft's *Riders Republic*, in which players take part in a climate march, and *Anno 1800*, which graphically illustrates the consequences of overdevelopment and environmental exploitation; and the ecological fables inherent in Giant Squid Studios' *ABZÛ* or ustwo's *Alba: A Wildlife Adventure*.

As Playmob's own survey of games studios shows, their appetite for further development in this direction is growing. Over 85% of companies surveyed want to run more campaigns and, as business environments increasingly focus on ESG, studios are more than ever inclined to support social and environmental causes – and organisations that value such causes beyond pure profit.

We have already looked at the types of activations games studios can leverage to make real-world impact, but they mainly fall into two categories: raise funds and raise awareness. These can go hand in hand as when you are raising funds for a cause, you are also educating people and raising awareness of the topic, but some studios may choose not to raise funds and only do awareness raising. For both, it is important to have a way to measure the impact and success. What have the funds raised contributed to? Have the messages landed enough to start nudging and changing behaviour in the right direction?

Raise funds

Fundraising has become an intrinsic part of gaming, whether it be through cause marketing or a game itself, or through donations from players or from the studio (from employees or rallying players together, or both). Children's charities have always been a firm favourite, but health and education, gender equality and environmental causes are becoming increasingly well supported, too.

Cause marketing is where players purchase an item in-game and a percentage of what they pay goes to a charity. Zynga was among the first studios to integrate cause marketing into games with its 2014 'Sweet Seeds For Haiti' campaign, which raised over $1.5 million in just five days.[101] Since then, many games have integrated items for sale to support causes, as can be seen by participants of the Green Game Jam.

Studios can also respond rapidly to crises and catastrophes across the world. When a devastating earthquake struck Turkey and Syria on 6 February 2023, Masomo, part of the Miniclip Group and based in Turkey, helped Miniclip identify aid organisations on the ground so it could pledge money towards them. Similarly, after the Black Lives Matter protests across the US in 2020, Niantic donated all its ticket revenues from the *Pokémon Go* Fest to black non-profits in affected urban areas to help them rebuild communities, as well as to fund black creators to develop stories and interactive experiences in support of the movement. In 2018, *Pokémon GO* creators Niantic organised an Earth Day initiative to engage players in marine conservation and pollution issues, delivering:

- 176 NGO hosted events and 300 player hosted events

- 41 countries and 6 continents

- 17,000 players volunteered 41,000 hours

- 145 tons of trash was collected

- Partnered with 46 NGOs[102]

'We find that people want to contribute to charity when we offer them the chance to do it,' says Richard Hatchett, CEO of Coalition of Epidemic Preparedness Innovations. 'It's not necessarily about redistributing money, but rather harnessing people's inner wish to do good deeds, and making it easy for them to do so.'

Increasingly, studios are realising that they can do more than simply write a one-off cheque for a charity, hold a public relations (PR) campaign around it and offset it against their tax bill. More and more studios are engaging their players in the fundraising effort by encouraging them to buy items in-game or make donations themselves. This collective action can inspire further action, and even just raising awareness of the cause can seed behaviour change, improving the lives of those potentially impacted by a crisis event, and of those playing and participating in the game.

As Robert Antokol, Founder and CEO of Playtika, says:

'I'm not saying it's easy, and the hardest thing
is to show the problem. What is the problem?
What problem is there? There are tons of
problems in the world. Some of them people
are not even aware of. Sometimes, you cannot
fix them, but you can speak about them –
and when you speak about them, solutions
can come.'

For Matt Fischer, Apple's Vice President of the App
Store, 'Apple's main purpose is to create products that
enrich people's daily lives. Having a positive impact
in the world is critical to our business, and we want
to leave the world in a better place than we found it.'

In the wake of the Covid pandemic, Rob Small
decided to set up a committee called Miniclip Gives,
which involved recruiting people from each of its
studios who are passionate about charity and about
trying to make positive impact and build a strategy
around charitable giving initiatives. One of the charities the initiative aligned with was Make A Wish,
which had good visibility, but didn't know how it
might intersect with the games industry.

Rob says:

'We asked a bunch of kids in devastating
situations what wish they would like to make
and they were so passionate about games that
they wanted something around games and
the games industry. One of the kids was mad
about *Mini Football*, so we created a character

in the game around that individual. It was
hugely exciting for the kid to come in and
meet us and see how the studio runs, and
then to actually be featured in the game –
and obviously great for us as a business to
be able to use some of our products to create
something special.'

Not only was Miniclip able to give funds to an important cause, but it also used its people's skills and
gaming magic to make a huge impact on a child who
was facing a traumatic experience.

Riot Games' first fundraising initiative was back in
2011, for the Red Cross, and it has recently created a
Social Impact fund that serves to deploy cash all over.
To date, it has supported thirty different causes raising $5.5m for them via the Give Back Bundle.

Call of Duty has an endowment, which was co-
founded by Bobby Kotick, CEO of Activision Blizzard,
and has raised almost $38m.[103] It exists to support war
veterans, from rehabilitation to helping them ease
back into communities, so the funds are strategically
aligned to support the very people represented in the
games. To date, the endowment has helped 100,000
veterans and generated an economic value of $5.6 bil-
lion in the US and UK.

There is an endless number of examples of funds
being raised through games and games studios, too
many to list here, but this is a flavour of the types
of games and studios donating to causes in different ways. An interesting piece of research would be

to analyse the amount raised from the industry and the impact generated. It would be a challenging piece of research, but it could enable studios to think more about the value of the impact – the 'so what?' – and really understand that activations are leading to a positive real-world impact.

Raise awareness

Rather than raising money directly, some games confront players with issues around climate change and environmental damage. Rob Small tells us:

> 'It's quite hard to weave in a narrative around environmental issues, and one needs to think carefully about it not being tokenistic. It really needs to fit in a meaningful way with the game format, rather than just being a label that's been slapped on the game for a short period.'

Decode Global Studio's mobile game *Get Water!*, for example, puts the player in the role of an Indian girl whose studies are constantly interrupted by the need to collect water, while Tunza Games' *Conservation Crisis* and *Little Chicken's Safari Central*[104] (in partnership with the organisation Internet of Elephants) teach about wildlife conservation. Other impact games feature storylines focused on the protection of the mangroves of Madagascar, sustainable urban planning in Kenya, wildlife conservation in Borneo, the global plight of the oceans and the effect of climate change through rising water levels on developing island states.

In 2014, the NGO Cybersmile partnered with Pixelberry Studios to deliver an in-game educational campaign around cyberbullying, based on the studio's highly successful *High School Story*.[105] In the game, players are armed with tools that empower them to know what to do in threatening situations. Cybersmile raised not only awareness, but also over $330,000 to support its work.

Another educational partnership saw *Minecraft* developers Mojang teaming up with the UN's Human Settlements Programme (UN-Habitat) on an innovative programme called Block by Block.[106] Through Block by Block, UN-Habitat uses *Minecraft* as a community participation tool in the design of urban public spaces. UN-Habitat's experience of implementing these projects all over the world shows that *Minecraft* is a good way of involving hard-to-reach youth, women and slum dwellers in urban design processes. It does this via distributing PCs loaded with copies of *Minecraft* to the village of Kibera in Kenya, with the aim of bringing the players' game-world urban blueprints to real life in public works in Kenya, Sweden and Haiti.[107] The game has sold nearly 100 million copies worldwide, making it one of the world's best-selling computer games.

Matt Fischer, Apple's Vice President of the App Store, sums up these attitudes: 'We want the characters in the games in our service to reflect the world we live in, and to embrace Apple's values.'

Respecting the art form

'For our consumer impact games, we lead with entertainment because we are competing for players' discretionary time (and dollars). The impact themes need to be organically aligned with a proven genre and compelling gameplay loops to ensure a competitive entertainment experience.'
— Alan Gershenfeld, President and Co-founder, E-Line Media

While studios increasingly want to incorporate green messaging and content into their games, they are aware of the danger of greenwashing – merely ticking boxes for PR or marketing purposes. The challenge – and it is a big one – is to do so in a genuine and sustainable way; in other words, to respect the art form that is gaming while using it for extrinsic (albeit laudable) ends.

Studios, partners and players alike should recognise that games cannot force people to do good; they can only point the way, enable and facilitate such actions. They can show – in a powerful way – the dangers of failing to do good and create (believable) alternatives to the status quo: aspirational but achievable futures. These possible futures that will inspire and motivate have been termed 'protopian' rather than utopian visions (as opposed to the dystopian visions increasingly peddled by the movie industry, for example).

For those wishing to work with the games industry, it is key to understand that the size of the industry does not always guarantee quick wins and there may be a period of testing, of trial and error, before you're able to do anything of scale. If you are looking to make a game, be mindful that not all games succeed. It is a craft better done by those who have done it before, who know the recipe, but even then, it is not a guaranteed success.

If you're working with existing games, there must be an alignment between the audience interests, the game theme and the objective and outcome of the activation. Shared alignment is key for in-game activations, for development of a new game and for elements surrounding games such as sponsorships in eSports. A well-thought-through collaboration will have a higher chance of success, and a well-thought-through test plan would not go amiss.

When delivering *Mission 1.5* to fifty-two countries, Playmob had to ensure not only that the topic and cultural alignment worked across all regions, but also that the technology could reach the audiences required. Before switching on the large roll out, the team tested in ten markets we were unsure about, reaching a small set of players and analysing the engagement and fall back rates (when an ad does not reach a player).

What we discovered was that the fall back rate was high due to the ad being a large file size. Those who played were engaging with the theme and content, so the issue that had to be fixed was a technical one. We made the file the smallest size possible then, upon the next roll out, the fall back rate was extremely small, meaning more people were reached. Had we not carried out this test, Playmob could have been in danger of not reaching the highest number of players possible.

The future of gaming

'It is about taking small steps, not being afraid that your business isn't hugely successful or huge scale yet. There's something that each of us can do and should do right now because we've been terrible custodians of the planet over the last thirty or so years. Quite frankly, we're stuffing the next generation with regard to the cost of getting through it all; it's a huge burden for them to carry on their shoulders. We owe it to them, not the games industry, to do something about it and make a positive step to make their lives slightly happier in the future.'
— Rob Small, President and Co-founder, Miniclip

We have touched on issues of player safety and security and the negative media image gaming has often attracted, as well as on the measures being taken by the industry to make the virtual world a safe playground for all. With the advent of AR and VR, of Web3 and the metaverse, games studios are looking to unlock new possibilities and turn them to their (competitive) advantage. Sadly, however, we are seeing many mistakes that happened twenty years ago happening again. Because anything is possible, anything often goes and the safety and security of players is being forgotten. As ever, there is a need for balance between freedom and responsibility; between moderating behaviour on the one hand and giving free rein to creatives and players on the other.

Rob Small believes there are interesting ways in which VR and AR can be leveraged, 'whether it's gamifying or educating kids through gameplay in schools or getting people thinking and interacting and engaging in world problems and possible solutions.' Marc Merrill, Co-chairman and Co-founder of Riot Games, expects game streaming – for example, through a TV – to significantly broaden the audience through narrative-driven games lasting a couple of hours instead of forty or more, with a combination of acting and live performance. This will enable the studios to reach people who aren't the 'hardcore gamers who are looking for the next *Fortnite* or whatever, but may just be looking for an interesting way to spend a couple of hours'.

The boom of Netflix gaming – and even Tesla having a games team – is beginning to bring games to new platforms and new experiences (not while driving, of course!) and really broaden out not just who plays, but how we play. The future and possibilities of where gaming can go are endless and we are only limited by our imaginations.

We have throughout the book referred to the issue of the industry's carbon footprint and mentioned the actions being taken to reduce it. One such action is currently being developed by Kara Stone, a designer and assistant professor at Alberta University of the Arts: a range of games that players will be able to stream (the first, *Known Mysteries*, is set in Canada, which in the game is at the mercy of big oil companies).[108] These games feature recycled visuals from 1970s industrial and nature films, compressed to fit on a tiny solar-powered web server on a Raspberry Pi microcomputer powered by an old car battery. Crazy? Maybe, but Stone's ideas challenge the accepted thinking that increasingly high-resolution graphics requiring ever-larger amounts of electricity and games that are fully accessible 24/7 are the inevitable future of the industry.

'Not everything has to be accessible to everybody at every single moment,' Stone says.

Some argue that these initiatives are merely a drop in the ocean and that radical ideas are needed if the games industry is to collectively decarbonise in the foreseeable future, as the Playing for the Planet Alliance hopes. According to Alan Gershenfeld, President and Co-founder of E-Line Media, the mixing of modalities between games, film/TV, graphic novels, education programmes and so on – what he calls the 'Marvelisation of impact media' or 'transmedia impact' – has enormous potential.

'Instead of a series of disparate, unconnected projects struggling to make impact in each of their domains, transmedia can take advantage of all these different media formats and enable them to play off each other. This is a huge opportunity and it is something that we're looking very closely at.'

Indeed, Gershenfeld envisages:

'...inspiring collective visions for evocative,
aspirational but achievable futures through
game-based communities that are a blend
of play and creation, which help us imagine
possible and preferred futures that we urge
into existence. That's a big, audacious,
wonderful goal that is possible.'

Marc Merrill has a similar vision:

'There's so much power and capability to
gather data and to reach different cohorts
or segments of the population through
technology, and to drive people or coordinate
communities towards more holistic goals,
that it's inevitable that gaming will evolve
in that direction. Figuring out how to wield
that power for good is going to be a really
interesting challenge.'

This view is echoed by John Hanke, CEO of Niantic,
who sees games as evolving towards social networks,
and social networks evolving towards games like
Fortnite and forums such as Reddit and Discord.

'It's about community and communication.
That's a powerful tool that can be positive or
negative. These can be places where there's
negativity or places where people find support

and friendship and positive reinforcement. We have to responsibly manage those online communities: they can accomplish incredibly positive things, but we can't just be neutral about it.'

Leading the way forward

'It depends a lot on the managers themselves, how they can split their time, how they can bring their personal agenda to bear.'
— Robert Antokol, Founder and CEO, Playtika

As the quotations dotted throughout this book show, the games industry is run by people who really care about their players, the planet and the future. In many cases, they set their companies up not simply as a quick way to make money, but because they want to make a difference and they recognise gaming as a way to do this; to inspire people to take action; to make games for all; to enable people to connect and have fun, get moving and exploring the great outdoors. They have all brought their own unique perspectives and motivations to the industry, and have done so in a way that can lead to a positive outcome for people and our planet.

John Hanke, for example, knew about research showing the benefits of a twenty-minute walk to boost mental health and wanted to create a way of getting people outdoors in nature or discovering culture and history. From the start, Niantic's mission was to do something that mattered and to build its products around that – products that could be commercially successful, but ultimately have a positive impact on the people who use them and the communities that they live in.

Rob Small, who was diagnosed with dyslexia at school, started his business because he found games an amazing escape. He observed first-hand the positive impact that games can have. From its inception, Miniclip's mission was 'to unleash the gamer in everyone' by removing all the obstacles that prevent people from getting into games – to the point of giving its games away for free.

Oliver Miao, Co-founder and Executive Advisor of Pixelberry, initially wanted to start an educational games company, but soon became aware of the tension between trying to educate people and do good while entertaining them. He decided instead to do what he and his team know how to do. The result was *High School Story*.

Robert Antokol has an even simpler ambition: 'to make people happier'. To make a game that would make people smile, because 'when you're smiling, you're feeling better'. He realised that if players were made to smile, they would keep coming back to the game and he would make money from it. He believed – and still believes – that 'if you give without asking, "What I will get from it?" you will always get more.'

Marc Merrill has always believed in service and philanthropy (he was an Eagle Scout), with a responsibility to help others and to give back – which became the mindset of Riot Games.

> 'We view our role as a company as serving our community; it's an online community primarily, but online people have offline lives. We all do. It's important not just to engage directly online, but also to do it again at the individual and the community level.'

It is clear that, however successful they become, such leaders never change their mindset – a mindset that they instil in their teams. When a leader has set the right tone and culture and empowered their teams, it shows, and it works. As Merrill says:

> 'The fluidity of expertise and team formation is something that tech companies, and gaming companies in particular, given the confluence of art and design and engineering and all the different skills that need to be brought to bear, can benefit enormously from. It's a very effective human collaboration model.'

Ilkka Paananen from Supercell has publicly announced that he wants to be the least powerful CEO in the industry. The way his business works – and the reason it is called Supercell – is that it is organised into independent games teams ('cells') that are empowered to make decisions, and the decision-making process is rapid. Not only does Supercell launch brilliant games, not only is it a multi-billion dollar games studio, but it has an empowered team, doing what they love in conditions which clearly enable people and business to thrive.

Culture is key. In the games industry more than in many others, it is about helping people to learn through letting them fail. Paananen even celebrates this culture by giving a bottle of champagne to the person who has had the biggest failure. The catch is that they have to talk about it – what went wrong and how the team can learn from it.

The games industry, as we have seen, has incalculable potential to do good. Gaming is already engaging billions of people and, as the industry's influence grows, so too will its ability to shape our future, but that potential cannot be unlocked unless the right culture and the right kind of leadership are in place. What is clear is that it will take brave, forward-thinking CEOs to pave the way and create opportunities that will continue to grow the positive impact potential of the industry and begin to solve some of the world's most pressing issues.

Bold moves have been taken on at Ubisoft, where the variable compensation of the CEO and deputy CEOs depends on whether the company reaches its carbon intensity reduction goals.[109] This is a huge step change not just for the games industry, but for all sectors – a rethink on incentivisation could be the solution to ensuring we hit our climate goals before it is too late. Protecting the planet should be rewarded as much as achieving a return for investors. If the planet is destroyed, then nothing else matters.

The more we can share the data around business impact from engaging players in positive actions, the more we can achieve as an industry. Impactful activations can enable a variety of roles to achieve KPIs, but only by sharing success stories, and things that did not work so well, can we then learn and build on successes to ensure that doing good is good for business too. There is still convincing to be done, but there is now enough data and momentum to convince. We just need to shout about it more and provide tools to make it easier for any studio to run activations.

Summary

- Start somewhere, no matter how small. Small actions collectively will make a big impact, while you learn about the process and build on the previous actions.

- Keep learning and growing the impact, whether you are raising funds or raising awareness, or both. Keep doing it and find ways to make these activities sustainable and part of the fabric of games.

- Respect the game – really understand what players want. If you're coming from outside of the industry, respect the art form and ensure contextual fit.

- Technological progress means that gaming will continue to evolve, and how we game will touch our lives more than we realise currently.

- The future will require brave, forward-looking leaders with a sense of responsibility and purpose, such as those we have heard from throughout this book.

- Grow your community spirit in the right direction, and when given a choice, choose right.

10
Good Gaming Guide

'It's not enough to say, "I've got 100,000 people playing a game." What needs to be asked is, "What happened to the players as a result? Did they change their behaviour?"'
— Asi Burak, Chairman, Games for Change and Chief Business Officer, Tilting Point

We have a lot to accomplish if we are to face global challenges head on and, in particular, the issue underpinning all issues: climate change. Gaming has enormous potential to make a difference, but how do we actually go about it?

This chapter gives some guidelines and principles for gamers, the gaming industry and the non-gaming industry that will point the way forward. We like to think of this as our manifesto for all: examples of actions we can strive to achieve to work together to make games as powerful as they can be, while being super fun and incredible experiences for players.

If you want your studio to make an impact through its games, what are the key things that you should be considering to achieve that? If you are a player, what kind of games should you be looking out for to learn and be inspired to take action, and how should you be changing your behaviours? If you run a platform, an app or game store, how should you be enabling more good to happen? How can you support unlocking the potential and making 'good' games more visible? If you are just interested in games in general – a spectator, a parent, a brand – what are the things you should be doing to help the industry to make the best use of its potential, while respecting the art form that is gaming? What can we all do, collectively, to make sure that games are used in the best and most appropriate way possible?

Our hope is that these guidelines become an inherent part of game production and the industry, and that cross-sector collaborations become simpler and more fruitful, for people, business and the planet.

Playing for good

'As a CEO, I'm not living in a bubble. I want the world around us to be better and I know that it is our obligation to make it better.'
— Robert Antokol, Founder and CEO, Playtika

As we saw from our analysis of over 200 games and gaming initiatives, there is a commitment across the industry to the SDGs in some capacity, although this is not always more widely appreciated. Even within the sector, day-to-day awareness of the SDGs, their relevance to the games industry and the role the industry could play in a global impact remains largely ignored, or is perceived as unimportant or not relevant. The leap has yet to be made in understanding that games *are* a powerful force for good and that sustainability credentials *are* good for business.

Our analysis will be updated in 2023 and a comparison between the first and the more recent study will show how much the industry has moved on in a very short space in time. We think the results will be surprising, especially as they will represent the time before and after Covid and the opening of the Playing for the Planet Alliance, along with the heightened awareness of the drastic action required to save our planet.

There is a need for highly coordinated efforts within the industry to lead the charge and further educate itself, players, other sectors and governments about the potential for gaming for good, which can then influence everything from day-to-day behaviour change to policy-level change. A leader board of impact mapped to the global goals could be a great way to showcase the work being done and instil a sense of healthy competition and partnership for the greater good of people and planet. What better way to incentivise the games industry than to give it rankings, achievements and challenges of its own in the biggest challenge of all – saving our precious planet and humanity?

Going green

We are discussing leveraging gaming to save the planet, and the more we play, the more good we can do. However, we do not want to solve a problem by creating another one equally detrimental to the planet.

The games industry is a significant contributor in the rise of e-waste, with consoles, computers and mobile devices being purchased and upgraded to play games, though reliable figures are hard to come by. According to Sony's 2021 sustainability report, its products alone generate over 17 million tons of CO_2 over their life cycle, with a further 14 million tons emitted from the company's offices and production facilities.[110]

Dr Ben Abraham of AfterClimate Solutions[111] has broken the problem down into four stages in the process of making games: emissions from game development, game distribution and sales, game play, and hardware manufacturing. If the games industry is to lead by example, it must of course make visible efforts to reduce its carbon footprint, which may not be as simple as it sounds.

As Nic Walker from Space Ape commented, 'We see the tip of the iceberg right now and we have a lot of work we need to do to better understand what lies beneath, for example, the carbon footprint of the ad networks we use.'

The industry is, nevertheless, taking meaningful steps to reduce its carbon footprint. Although games can still be bought in a box, this is less and less common as downloading becomes the norm. For those games that are sold in stores, companies are switching to renewable materials for their packaging. Sega, for example, is now using paper and cardboard rather than plastic and cellophane. PlayStation and Xbox are also making positive moves in this area. Elsewhere, researchers are working on solar-powered web servers.

According to Ben Abraham, Nintendo makes one of the most efficient gaming devices of this generation[112] and seems aware of the need to act to reduce its impact. Nearly everyone is working hard – a lot of it behind the scenes. The crucial thing now is accelerating the pace of change.

Games companies are also looking at the wider impact of the industry on the climate. In January 2020, the Microsoft CFO, Amy Hood, stood up and announced publicly that the business would be carbon negative by 2030[113] – without actually knowing how this would be achieved.

CEO of Gaming at Microsoft, Phil Spencer, explains, 'We've got sight lines on about 80% of what that means; the other 20% we've got to invent in the next decade,' but the challenge is both 'invigorating' and good PR. 'Our customers see a transparency and an authenticity in being public about what our aspiration is.'

Xbox now offers carbon-aware downloads and updates. This means when a console is plugged in, connected to the internet, and regional emissions data are available, downloads and updates will occur at times when a 'higher proportion of electricity is coming from lower-carbon sources on the electric grid'. Microsoft has also launched a toolkit which will measure real-time Xbox energy use.[114] Game makers on the Xbox platform will now be able to experiment with ways to reduce their games' energy consumption.

Google Play is decarbonising its energy consumption with the aim of operating exclusively on carbon-free energy by 2030. The business is also actively supporting water security and ecosystems wherever it operates and has pledged to replenish 120% of the water it consumes by 2030.

Rovio ensures its players' emissions are included in its own greenhouse gas accounting, adding an 'additional emission category' for 'device energy use of [its] YouTube viewers'. For players, it 'changed the calculation model to be based on actual play/view time instead of the previous rough assumption of one daily active user consuming a full battery a day'.[115]

Supercell has attempted to calculate its overall carbon footprint as a business and shared its learning with other companies through the Playing for the Planet Alliance (Chapter 6).[116] Space Ape has taken on this plan and is attempting to build on it, as are many other studios, and then share its progress through groups and alliances that have their own guides and support for studios, such as UKIE[117] and NeoGames.[118]

Rob Small, President and Co-founder of Miniclip, is 'not convinced that anyone's properly nailed how to calculate their carbon footprint', but he remains cautiously optimistic:

'We need to establish what our big goals are, and establish some KPIs to measure our footprint as a business in a more meaningful way. We're on this journey to do as much as we can and we'll continue down that road and hopefully make a greater and greater contribution to [saving the planet].'

According to Ben Abraham of AfterClimate Solutions, there is 'heaps' more the industry can do:

'It can electrify heating, cooling and vehicle fleets. It can improve the energy efficiency of software and hardware – energy efficiency often gets overlooked, but at the scale of the games industry, shaving even a few watts off a new console or off the work done in massive data centres can add up to significant emissions savings. Companies can purchase renewable electricity, and bigger companies can make power-purchase agreements that enable the building of new renewable power generation plants. The industry can also make game hardware last longer and make games for platforms with lower energy profiles (like mobile and Switch). A lot of changes are possible even without compromising too much on the experience for players.'

Beyond internal changes, games companies are encouraging players to go green not only by reducing their footprint when gaming, but also by supporting initiatives such as tree-planting. They are also encouraging players to think about their behaviours and actions – not only while playing – such as using public transport rather than driving. The International Game Developers Association has developed an Environmental Game Design Playbook,[119] which helps game designers to think about how to create a green activation in-game or a game about environmental issues. As we've discussed, a game or game content designed to teach players about a topic must be led with fun first or people won't play it.

For Abraham, players themselves have a responsibility to:

> '…make a noise. They should ask the people
> who make their favourite games what they are
> doing about reducing their carbon footprint,
> ask for more details and information about
> the carbon embedded in the games they play,
> whether the servers they play on are powered
> by renewables, and so on. Maybe one day,
> games will have a label on them to explain
> what each one has cost the planet and we can
> choose to play better ones…'

Leveraging existing games with existing audiences is a much quicker and more scalable way to reach gamers, and organisations are building solutions to do just this. Platforms such as Games Forest Club activate gamers to plant trees, while PlanetPlay enables them to offset their carbon footprint across a range of impactful projects, as well as giving other benefits back to players such as discounts on IAPs, downloadable content (DLC) and games. Over time, we foresee more platforms coming into the industry to support impactful activations, enabling games studios to do more, generate more impact, without it being a time- or resource-intensive activity. It is early days for these types of platforms, but if the industry works collaboratively with new technologies, there is a great opportunity to create solutions which can be transformational.

Platforms that remove the heavy lifting of building impactful activations in-game, bringing business uplift as well as a positive ROI for the planet, will be the ones that unlock the huge opportunity for the industry to solve the climate crisis. They will take the impact beyond reducing or removing carbon footprint to gaming being a hero, tackling the crisis head on and paving the way forward for the whole tech sector.

Sharing goals

'The games industry has a unique opportunity to design evocative, aspirational but achievable visions of the future to inspire gamers, individually and collectively, to then urge them into reality.'
— Alan Gershenfeld, President and Co-founder, E-Line Media

We have talked about the Playing for the Planet Alliance and the Green Game Jams (see Chapter 6), which have brought different industry players together to share their knowledge and ideas. There are also other industry collaborations, such as the Play Fair Alliance[120] and the Play Apart Together initiative launched during the Covid-19 pandemic.[121] This was an initiative in collaboration with the WHO, which had moved on from a standpoint of talking about gaming disorder to actually embracing games during the pandemic. The initiative leveraged games as a way to reach people and give information and reminders to stay safe.

In our experience, it is motivational for studios to actually see the joint impact they can make when they work together. Every year, for example, the Playing for the Planet Alliance publishes an impact report, which shows what the industry as a whole has achieved. You might run a small studio that has planted 1,000 trees, which is admirable, but when you see that collectively the industry has planted 10 million trees, it is likely to motivate you to do more because you are part of a larger effort. You may be playing a small part, but it is contributing to something big.

One example of the industry working together is GamesAid, a UK charity supporting causes from money raised by a variety of games companies.[122] Humble Bundle is a digital store selling donated games on a 'pay-what-you-want' model; purchasers even specify the percentage they wish to go to charity, which averages over 30%.[123]

The essential thing for the industry to do is to look at how and where it can make the most impact. Which are the most powerful levers that it can pull and how should it encourage studios to step up to the plate? Is this in game design, new business models, partnerships or rallying audiences on social media? The question isn't how impact can be implemented, the question is when – the sooner we start, the sooner we learn, iterate and improve.

Making it work

> 'How we steer the games industry in a direction that will help to create more positivity and impact is going to be fascinating to observe over the next few years, A lot of the younger people in our organisations feel extremely passionate about it. They're going to be CEOs of businesses in the next decade and this is going to be at the forefront of their minds. Once they unleash that potential, it's going to be extremely exciting to see what's possible.'
> — Rob Small, President and Co-founder, Miniclip

In general – perhaps even simplistic – terms, what works is what comes out of a genuine effort to do good. If we focus on the outcome of genuine impact, then the player enjoyment and business uplift will follow.

As we have seen, an emphasis on ESG is starting to build in the games industry, but it has not quite come to the surface yet, as businesses are still focused on business results. Although there are many examples of CEOs leading from the front (including all those who have contributed to this book), there are still people within the industry who need a little more convincing of the business case for doing good.

These people need hard evidence and simple arguments. Strong-arming is a waste of time, as is presenting them with a shopping list of goals. They may be reluctant to introduce yet another thing into their games and, indeed, may not have the time or confidence to do so; they may need to create an implementation team to make it easy for them or trust that third-party platforms can do the job for them.

We have also seen that simply pasting an environmental theme or message on to an existing game is counterproductive because players will see through it immediately. It is therefore essential that the industry really understands what players care about, what works for them and what is going to excite them. If they do the proper research, studios have an opportunity to start nudging even the most sceptical people in the right direction.

This means looking at the activations that have already been achieved, player profiles and game genres to find the best matches for studios and games that are wanting to do something around, say, climate change. Should it be a fundraiser, a storyline, a new item or character, or purely messaging that is put into the game? What are players going to enjoy and engage with most?

There is a gap in this research currently, but visibility and knowledge will equip studios with more confidence and evidence of what could work for them. In fact, it may be something we build on from this book, which can then generate practical guides and implementation solutions aligned with a variety of game genres, audiences, impact goals and outcomes.

Level of involvement	Type of integration	Integration details
High	Themed games	The entire game is dedicated to a particular theme or topic. The game is built from scratch.
High	AR/VR	Specific (threatened) ecosystems or animals are bought to life through an up-close-and-personal immersive experience. The games are built from scratch.
Medium	Environments/ Levels	A realistic environment or new level in a game conveys its own narrative.
Medium	Integrated storylines	A scenario is played out to simulate outcomes or stimulate discussion.
Medium	Characters	The characters convey positive views or opinions, eg, 'I always recycle.'
Light	In-game items	Players are encouraged or incentivised to choose 'good' items (eg, hybrid cars in racing games, low-energy consumer items in homes) or penalised for poor choices or actions taken.

(Continued)

(Cont.)

Level of involvement	Type of integration	Integration details
Light	In-game text/ messages	In-game messages encouraging positive environmental behaviours, such as turning off engines while idling or devices when not in use. Could use in-game chat or message systems.
Light	In-game purchases	Purchases, such as IAPs, DLC, game download, support a charity partner with real-world impact.
Light	In-game milestones	Achieve a milestone such as reach level 10, and unlock the impact, eg, a corporate donation to a cause.
No integration	In-game advertising	Advertised items subsidised or offered free in support of awareness days (eg, World Environment Day, Earth Day, World Oceans Day) or specific campaigns, or only advertise pro-environmental messages and brands, or % of advertising revenue goes to environmental projects.
No integrations	Social media	Players are encouraged to share messages around impactful behaviours. Games have large communities on social channels to share actions and messages with.
No integrations	Donations	A share of revenue from sales is donated to a charity partner.

Games Impact Canvas

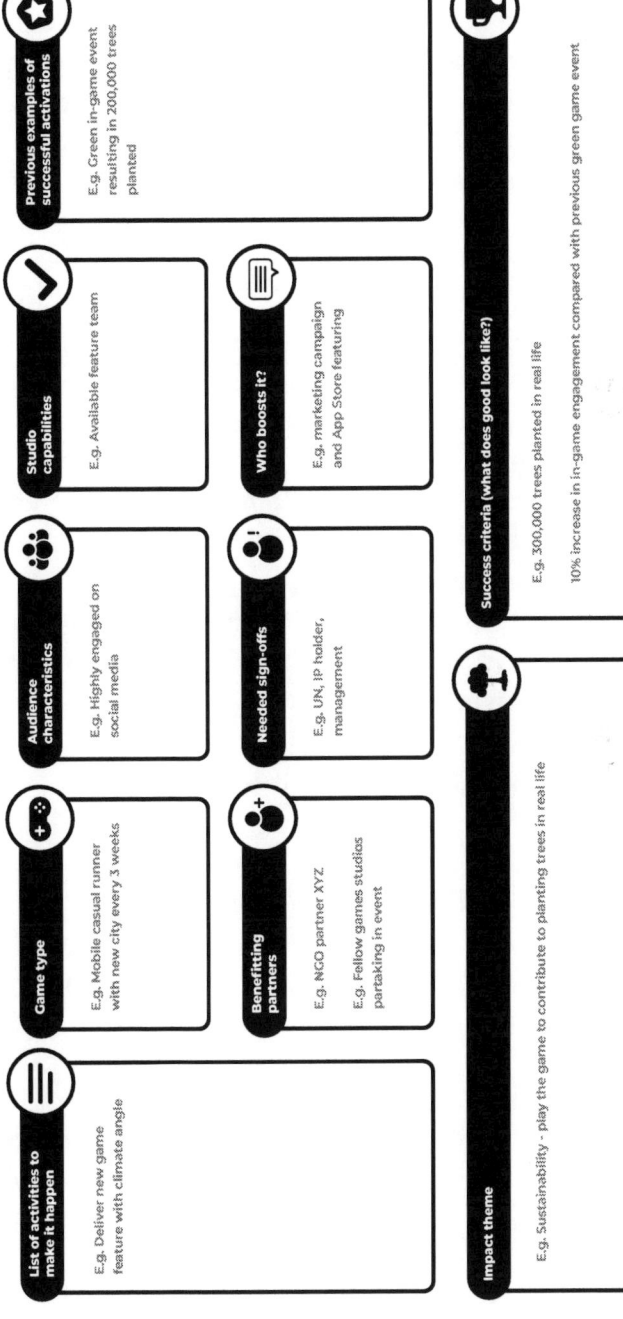

List of activities to make it happen
E.g. Deliver new game feature with climate angle

Game type
E.g. Mobile casual runner with new city every 3 weeks

Audience characteristics
E.g. Highly engaged on social media

Studio capabilities
E.g. Available feature team

Previous examples of successful activations
E.g. Green in-game event resulting in 200,000 trees planted

Benefitting partners
E.g. NGO partner XYZ
E.g. Fellow games studios partaking in event

Needed sign-offs
E.g. UN, IP holder, management

Who boosts it?
E.g. marketing campaign and App Store featuring

Impact theme
E.g. Sustainability - play the game to contribute to planting trees in real life

Success criteria (what does good look like?)
E.g. 300,000 trees planted in real life
10% increase in in-game engagement compared with previous green game event

Games Impact Canvas

As we saw in Chapter 1, gamers are not a single demographic; they are everyone. Reaching the right people with the right message needs careful thought, and again, a balance must be maintained between achieving an impact and delivering an enjoyable gaming experience. The flow of the game must not be interrupted; players must be constantly challenged and be able to see (and share) their achievements and progress. The more serious the message, the more fun the game needs to be – and make sure that there is a feedback loop, so that player engagement (with both the game and the issue at stake) can be monitored and the experience constantly refined and optimised.

To support studios in their thinking about all the aspects of integrating activations in-game, we have created the Games Impact Canvas which outlines the various elements of an activation to get initial thoughts flowing and structured. This canvas may evolve over time, but from where we are today, it covers key requirements of an activation.

Practical steps and advice

To end this chapter, we have summarised some practical steps for the games industry, gamers, policy makers and other sectors, in terms of how they can be part of unlocking the huge potential of games to do good. We have also highlighted some expert opinions from those we've interviewed for this book – with centuries of combined experience and 'stripes earned' between them, their guidance is second to none.

Games industry

- Start from within – educate employees on impact-related topics, bring in experts to run sessions and enable your staff to integrate socially good actions into their roles, to combine doing good with reaching KPIs.

- Listen internally – find out what your teams care about and align impact initiatives with their areas of interest. This will help you not only retain great people, but also attract employees to the organisation.

- Empower your teams – giving responsibility to a few or a group to run with socially good initiatives without having to wade through layers of approvals will not only help your organisation move faster, but also make your teams feel rewarded and trusted.

- Tackle your carbon footprint – use the guidelines we've discussed to better understand your footprint. This will then help you to define goals and targets, when you are ready.

- In-game activations – just start! There is so much to learn and there are so many variations to how these are done, we suggest you pilot ideas and grow and refine over time. Here is some advice to get you started:

- Use our Games Impact Canvas to think about all the various elements.

- Talk to expert platforms such as PlanetPlay that do the heavy lifting of implementing activations if you are time and resource constrained.

- Share your results. Only by sharing our knowledge can we as an industry better understand what works/doesn't work and continually improve.

- Work on making activations sustainable and ongoing rather than one-offs. This reduces the time and effort for your studio as well as generating a bigger impact.

- Listen externally – what do your players care about and want to support? Bring this into your game design and activations while better understanding how you can use this data to make real-world change.

- Share, share, share! Join alliances such as Playing for the Planet, and networks and share your learnings and expertise. One single organisation will not solve these issues alone, we need to join forces to solve them together.

- Engage parents in understanding the importance of games-for-good and support them to create healthy habits for their children by providing resources, expertise and ideas.

- Partnerships – work with local or regional government, multi-sector organisations, NGOs or industry competitors and develop innovative partnerships that allow good initiatives to scale and encourage collaboration across companies.

Gamers

- Play good games – look for games that do good, promote them and encourage them to keep doing good work.

- Speak up – tell the makers of the games you love to do more for the planet. The games studios will listen and take on board what you care about. Leverage your favourite games to speak up and look for opportunities, such as *Mission 1.5*, to have your voice heard by decision makers.

- Climate clans – in multiplayer games, create groups in support of the planet or environmental causes and bring together like-minded players to learn and take action. We can't tackle these issues on our own.

- Take control – organise a fundraiser on a live-stream for a cause you care about.

- Participate in game-a-thons and hack-a-thons that encourage idea generation and collaboration in support of important causes, and utilise gaming as a positive means to share information and educate your communities.

- Share – if you do good through games, share your positive actions to raise awareness of the cause, as well as the good you have done as a player and the game.

- Commitments – make your own commitments and change little things which can become daily habits. For example, power down your console, switch off lights, wash your clothes at a lower temperature, etc.

- Reuse and recycle – buy second-hand consoles and games (if you use boxed products) and when you are done with them, sell them on or give them to someone who could benefit.

Other sectors (NGOs, brands, influencers, etc)

- The right fit – look for games partners who share your vision and impact goal, and find the person who manages their impact to have the initial conversation. They will be your biggest ambassador.

- Size matters – target games with a large audience. Without an audience, any activation efforts would just waste time. Even if the game does have an audience, ensure you understand the player base and their likes/dislikes. Appealing to the players is key, but of course there needs to be players to appeal to!

- Uplift – better understand the models and KPIs of the games industry, in particular the studios and games you wish to collaborate with as they will move quicker if your proposals are aligned with their business outcomes.

- Roadmaps – get to know the studios and their roadmap cycles. Once you know what is happening and when, you can build out a plan together.

- Halo effects – studios love to be in the limelight and will try out innovative ways to attract new players and bring back disengaged players.

- Test small before going big – start in one market and review results – both player responses and technically – before expanding.

- Keep in context – make sure you have aligned with the right type of game and audience for the collaboration you wish to make. Something which is out of context will look odd to players and they may not engage. Even worse, they could lash back against it.

- Fun, fun, fun – don't forget that collaborations with games studios must be fun and light touch. Gamers are playing a game for a reason – they want to play that game. The activation will be new to them and perhaps something they have not considered, so keep it fun and high level so they can engage and enjoy, and then go back to playing the host game.

Advice from the experts

Alan Gershenfeld, President and Co-founder of E-Line Media, emphasises the importance of rigour in game development:

'Any time we move into a project, we start with a landscape and opportunity analysis. Here, we look at all the other projects that have attempted to do something similar in games and other media, and really understand what's worked, what hasn't worked, what is working, what could potentially work. Who are the stakeholders in this project? Are the stakeholders aligned on their impact objectives, their financial objectives, their risk tolerance, the process?

'This is upfront work that needs to be done because often there is misalignment and even misunderstanding. A mobile social game of service is very different from a console game as a product. They have totally different design, development and publishing methodologies, so I would say my biggest piece of advice is to go through that rigorous process.'

A similar approach, Gershenfeld says, is required when you're assessing the potentially negative impacts of a game:

'Most folks in the games for change space just look at the positives, but whether it's too much screen time, whether it's a culture of violence or misogyny, whether it's toxic communities, whether it's predatory business models, these are all things that need to be studied and understood. They're very complex things and there are no simple answers.'

When it comes to human resources, Gershenfeld advises that we must realise games are 'a craft, not a commodity. You need great game designers and you need a number of different projects, because you never know for sure which ones are going to work.' It is essential to recruit 'the most talented creatives, whether they're design directors, lead programmers or art directors, and especially those that can lead teams. It all starts with the talent and the passion.'

Matt Fischer, Apple's Vice President of the App Store, offers advice that chimes with Alan Gershenfeld's view. 'Work hard, bring passion to everything you do, be curious and surround yourself with people smarter than you.'

Marc Merrill, Co-chairman and Co-founder of Riot Games, prioritises diversity of talent and has set up a fund to invest in and support development teams and gaming companies that are led by women and under-represented minorities. 'We don't want to just pull great employees from diverse backgrounds. We're taking a much more upstream view to increase the supply so that everybody can find the right company or fit.'

Rob Small, President and Co-founder of Miniclip, points to the talent war:

> '[This] has gone on over the last few years, with unbelievable salary inflation, particularly in Europe. There are a lot of choices out there now, but it's about more than just negotiating the best package. A lot of employees are asking themselves, "What kind of company do I really want to work for?" The answer is, a company that is behaving in a way that is aligned with their personal thoughts and beliefs.'

With regard to the tension between what might make a good game and what is good for business, Small's number-one piece of advice is: 'Don't be afraid.' Fear is probably the biggest factor in executives or companies as a whole failing to innovate. The challenges can seem insurmountable, but:

> '…you don't need to solve climate change all by yourself tomorrow. Start small, try some things to engage your employees, talk to people, put one foot in front of the other. One of my favourite quotes is from Gandhi, who said that the enemy is fear. The most destructive behaviours I've seen or personally experienced are often driven by fear, so just have courage.

'It's overwhelming sometimes, the size of the hurdle. I do worry that the scale of the problem means that people shy away from it. What we've learned at Miniclip is you need to start building the dialogue, and then the dialogue needs to turn to action. Small steps are a good place to start. We're not going to solve this overnight, so let's just get on the road, get on the journey.'

At the same time, Small believes that 'businesses need to take a lead in helping to shape and organise mass volunteer efforts if they really want to make an impact.' Partnerships with NGOs are also crucial, and these can start with a chat over lunch:

'It's an easy thing to do and it really helps to plant that seed with NGOs and with charities to try to move things forward on their own. It's a great way for them to learn; the employees feel good because they're sharing knowledge and it makes them feel they're adding value.'

For Oliver Miao, Co-founder and Executive Advisor of Pixelberry, it is equally important to involve the business's own employees.

'If leaders are actually listening to their employees, they'll discover that there are so many people in gaming companies who really care. They're passionate about games, they're

passionate about other things in their lives and they want to make a difference themselves.
They want their work to be meaningful, so it's not hard for leaders to do [good]; it's simply a matter of unlocking all that passion and power within their companies.'

John Hanke, CEO of Niantic, echoes Miao's advice: 'For companies to be competitive, they're going to have to find ways that allow people to align their non-work persona with their work persona to accomplish things that they consider meaningful.' It is vital to listen to customers and understand what they want. 'Where are they getting value in the product? What new things do they want us to do?'

Hanke also believes that studios:

'…need to lead and anticipate things that may not be immediately obvious to our players. Ultimately, even though people didn't really know that they wanted it, they liked it and it made them happy about the game, happy about spending time with it and enthusiastic about sharing it with their friends. Part of it is looking for those insights where you can deliver something that's both going to be positively received and going to have a good impact.

'The first thing is for us as an industry to do no harm; to ask ourselves what patterns, what behaviours, what cultural stereotypes, what activities is our product actually putting out there? It's a big world, so everybody has to ask themselves, "How can we leverage the power that we have – the company, the resources, the user base, the product design – to have the maximum impact?"'

Phil Spencer, CEO of Gaming at Microsoft, poses similar questions:

'Do people feel that they are represented in the games that we're building? Can they find the right players to play with? Can they create a safe and inclusive place for them and their family to play in? What tools and technologies and capabilities do we need to give people the right kind of canvas to express themselves in a safe way?

'It's critically important that as an industry, we understand what our customers want to see from us and make sure that they feel the companies they're investing in are representing their points of view. It's not about getting everything right, it's about growing and learning and getting better.'

For Marc Merrill, gaming can actively reinforce good behaviours. Over the next five to ten years, the industry will develop much more effective standards, practices and technology to help reinforce positive play – for example, by making it cool to be a good guy or by players earning a credit score so that reputation matters. Riot Games has created an Instant Feedback Tool, whereby players can report another player for bad behaviour or honour them for good behaviour.

> 'You get kudos for being a good teammate and random rewards to reinforce that positive behaviour that people want. If you're getting reported for not being a great player to work with, once you hit a particular threshold, you will get a report card that gives you tips and tools for improving your behaviour.'

In extreme cases, players can be prevented from chatting with other people in game for a limited amount of time or even banned from a game altogether.

> 'What's great is, we found that 70% of players who get a report card don't have any issues ever again – which demonstrates that we are teaching them that there are other people on the other end and having an online identity doesn't mean there aren't consequences in real life.'

Rachel Franklin, SVP of Positive Play at EA, advises:

> 'Think about how we can encourage people to be kind *and* competitive. Positive play is not about making everything G rated. It's about helping make sure players fulfil their motivation when they set out to play. Do they

want to compete? Or create? Or connect? Or find friends? You can do all of that while still being kind and fun.'

Ilkka Paananen, CEO and Co-founder of Supercell, sums up the advice quoted above:

'We need to make our virtual communities safe for all kinds of players from different backgrounds. The most important thing is just to get the discussion going within your own company, in your own teams, and find out what people care about and what the company could do better in its games. Then grow it from there. It's so much about enabling your own people to do amazing things. The vast majority of people want to do the right thing and they want to do good, but we have to make sure that the companies actually enable that.'

As does Tamzin Taylor, Head of Google Play Partnerships in Western Europe:

'Get involved. If you're a game developer, join the Playing for the Planet Alliance; look at what commitments your own studio can make; participate in the Green Game Jam; and think about where it makes sense for your game to incorporate a sustainability message. It has to fit in with your game and your players, rather than be tacked on top and unrelated to game play. With game developers joining initiatives like Playing for the Planet, we'll see more opportunities to create truly scaled global action.'

Rob Small puts it in a nutshell. 'Consumers care deeply about many of these issues now and expect the businesses that they buy products from or interact with to share some of their values.'

Summary

- We must continue to build on the efforts that games for good have achieved so far with collaborations from industry, the players and even policy makers.

- Going green is a huge topic and action for any games studio of any size today. Our heightened awareness of our footprint means we understand that being digital does not mean being green.

- Sharing results is key to enable others to build on learnings and encourage more to participate – evidence of in-game activations being good for business will help build the business case for good!

- Doing more research on activations, drawing conclusions and building on these results to keep improving and optimising, will enabling us to create a handbook or detailed guide on what works well for particular games, genres and audiences.

- Our practical steps for games studios, players and industry are a great place to start, but of course they're not exhaustive and can be built on as we all learn.

- The advice from the seasoned experts interviewed in this book is gold. This is decades of experience, summarised and passed on to you, our readers, to take forth and make great games and game activations, to do good!

Conclusion

Games are a unique medium for two-way com-munication on a massive scale, but they are also entertainment. They tap into a fundamental aspect of being human – the need for play, which triggers emotions and behaviours that can have significant consequences. They also take up a considerable share of mind, which is hugely powerful if we want to change the world and make it better for all.

This book has shone a spotlight on the power games can have by their pure global nature, speed to reach people, and the diversity and inclusivity of the audiences playing – almost 50% of the world's population. It has included examples, showcasing how games can be a powerful force for good, whether it's by studios creating bespoke games or leverag-ing existing ones, depending on what action and output is required. There are many great case studies out there and this book has helped us realise that a directory of examples and activations would be an extremely useful resource for the world to inspire further action. From raising awareness to having a voice on the political agenda, games can be used as a communication tool, engaging with people from Dundee to Djibouti on topics that matter to them and to all of us without taking away the fun.

Gamers are adept at solving complex problems in real time, collaborating with strangers to achieve common goals and adapting rapidly to new technologies. These skills, if deployed at scale and applied to critical issues like climate change, global poverty and gender equality, could radically change the face of the world as we know it today. We hope this book has demystified the games industry and shown the huge potential to be unlocked.

Our goal was to reinforce this potential with the industry itself, make it proud of its achievements to date and show what more can be done and is within its power to do. To show gamers that they can be empowered to make real-world change just by playing, and by letting their favourite games makers know they want this. This will unlock more positive action in-game. For those not in the industry, it may be an eye-opener for them to better understand that games are not just a pastime, but are a hugely powerful cultural megatrend, potentially the biggest of our time. We must use this power and influence to point the world in the right direction.

The gaming industry has the potential to be an integral partner in solving global issues and achieving the SDGs in the little time we have left to achieve them. It supplies essential cause-related data around what people care about and where and how they want to take action, and provides real-world activities that will enable them to do so.

The actions we have looked at in this book are merely the tip of the iceberg; the possibilities for using games for good are far greater than we might imagine. As gaming becomes integral to our daily lives, we must ensure that we make the best use of it. There are many challenges to be faced, but there is an enormous collective will – on the part of the industry, the players and those on the outside looking in – to overcome them so that gaming is a positive force for both people and the planet.

We are literally playing for our lives.

Notes

1   UNDP, *The Peoples' Climate Vote* (UNDP, 2021), www.
    undp.org/publications/peoples-climate-vote, accessed
    29 June 2023
2   IPCC, *Climate Change 2022: Impacts, Adaptation and
    Vulnerability* (IPCC, 2022), www.ipcc.ch/report/ar6/wg2,
    accessed 7 July 2023
3   J McGonigal, *Reality is Broken: Why games make us better and
    how they can change the world* (Vintage, 2012)
4   C Ferguson, PM Markey, *Moral Combat: Why the war on
    violent video games is wrong* (BenBella Books, 2017)
5   IPCC, *Climate Change 2023 Synthesis Report: Summary for
    policymakers* (IPCC, 2023), www.ipcc.ch/report/ar6/syr/
    downloads/report/IPCC_AR6_SYR_SPM.pdf, accessed
    29 June 2023
6   Statista, *Video Games – Worldwide* (2023), www.statista.com/
    outlook/dmo/digital-media/video-games/worldwide,
    accessed 1 July 2023
7   Statista, *Distribution of Video Gamers in the United States in
    2022, By age group* (Statista, no date), www.statista.com/
    statistics/189582/age-of-us-video-game-players, accessed
    1 July 2023

8 Ofcom, *Adults' Media Use and Attitudes report, 2020/21*, www.ofcom.org.uk/__data/assets/pdf_file/0025/217834/adults-media-use-and-attitudes-report-2020-21.pdf, accessed 1 July 2023

9 GWI, *Report: The Gaming Playbook* (GWI, no date), www.gwi.com/reports/the-gaming-playbook, accessed 1 July 2023

10 *Women in Games: About page*, www.womeningames.org/about-us, accessed 1 July 2023

11 M Ball, *The Metaverse: And how it will revolutionize everything* (Liveright, 2022)

12 Newzoo, *Top Countries/Markets by Game Revenues* (Newzoo, 2023), https://newzoo.com/insights/rankings/top-10-countries-by-game-revenues, accessed 1 July 2023

13 M Barr, A Copeland-Stewart, 'Playing video games during the COVID-19 pandemic and effects on players' well-being', *Sage Journals*, Volume 17, Issue 1 (2021), https://doi.org/10.1177/15554120211017036, accessed 29 June 2023

14 J Koetsier, 'The top 50 mobile games of 2023 (so far)' (singular, 2023), www.singular.net/blog/top-mobile-games, accessed 27 July 2023

15 T Gu, '2021's mobile market: Almost four billion smartphone users, \$90.7 billion in game revenues and huge changes to come', Newzoo (23 September 2021), https://newzoo.com/resources/blog/2021s-mobile-market-almost-four-billion-smartphone-users-90-7-billion-in-game-revenues-huge-changes-to-come, accessed 5 July 2023

16 Awful Announcing, '82.98 billion mobile game downloads in 2021, but which sports titles are best?' (2 March 2022), https://awfulannouncing.com/gaming/82-98-billion-mobile-game-downloads-in-2021-but-which-sports-titles-are-best.html, accessed 10 August 2023

17 B Jovanovic, 'Gamer Demographics: Facts and stats about the most popular hobby in the world', DataProt (25 May 2023), https://dataprot.net/statistics/gamer-demographics, accessed 10 August 2023

18 Fortune, *Gaming Console Market Size, Share & Industry Analysis, By Type (Home Consoles and Handheld Console (Portable and Non-Portable)), By End-use (Residential and Commercial), By Applications (Gaming and Non-Gaming), and Region Forecast, 2020–2027* (Fortune Business Insight, no date), www.fortunebusinessinsights.com/gaming-console-market-102420, accessed 1 July 2023

19 J Clement, 'Number of PC gaming users worldwide from 2008 to 2024', Statista (2023), www.statista.com/statistics/420621/number-of-pc-gamers, accessed 1 July 2023

20 K Cieślak, 'REPORT: Women and games – how do modern female gamers play?', try_evidence (7 February 2022), https://tryevidence.com/blog/report-women-and-games-how-do-modern-female-gamers-play, accessed 10 August 2023

21 TXH, 'What are the most popular game genres that are played in 2022' (2022), www.thexboxhub.com/what-are-the-most-popular-game-genres-that-are-played-in-2022, accessed 1 July 2023

22 Newzoo, *Most Popular PC Games By Monthly Active Users – Global* (2023), https://newzoo.com/insights/rankings/top-20-pc-games, accessed 1 July 2023

23 Statista, *Breakdown of US Computer and Video Game Sales from 2009 to 2017, By Delivery Format* (2019), www.statista.com/statistics/190225/digital-and-physical-game-sales-in-the-us-since-2009, accessed 30 December 2018

24 J McGonigal, *Reality is Broken: Why games make us better and how they can change the world* (Vintage, 2012)

25 M Gardner, 'Here's how many years of your life you sacrifice to gaming', *Forbes* (18 December 2020), www.forbes.com/sites/mattgardner1/2020/12/18/how-much-of-your-life-you-sacrifice-to-gaming-in-years/?sh=2c28408946be, accessed 10 August 2023

26 V Combs, '8 hours and 27 minutes. That's how long the average gamer plays each week', TechRepublic (10 March 2021), www.techrepublic.com/article/8-hours-and-27-minutes-thats-how-long-the-average-gamer-plays-each-week, accessed 15 November 2023

27 M Dimitrievski, 'Gaming Statistics – 2023', True List (25 February 2023), https://truelist.co/blog/gaming-statistics, accessed 10 August 2023

28 J Jakob, '80% of Gen Z and Millennial consumers play games', *Newzoo* (5 August 2021), https://newzoo.com/resources/blog/consumer-data-gen-z-millennials-baby-boomer-gen-x-engagement-games-esports-metaverse, accessed 5 July 2023

29 S Domsch, *Storyplaying: Agency and narrative in video games,* (De Gruyter, 2013); G Frasca, 'Rethinking agency and immersion: Video games as a means of consciousness-raising', *Digital Creativity*, 12(3) (2001) 167–74

30   RM Ryan; EL Deci, 'Intrinsic and extrinsic motivations: Classic definitions and new directions', *Contemporary Educational Psychology*, 25(1) (2000) 54–67

31   D Mensah-Bonsu et al, 'Green Game Jam Player Survey 2022', Playing for the Planet Alliance (2022), https://www.playing4theplanet.org/post/ggj22-survey, accessed 31 July 2023

32   L Rees, '2022: The games market in numbers', *PocketGamer. biz* (2022), www.pocketgamer.biz/special-report/80497/the-games-market-will-generate-1844-billion-in-2022-with-mobile-leading-the-way, accessed 1 July 2023

33   Statista, *Video Games – Worldwide* (2023), www.statista.com/outlook/dmo/digital-media/video-games/worldwide, accessed 1 July 2023

34   Graphic by Visual Capitalist in article: O Wallach, '50 Years of Gaming History, by Revenue Stream (1970–2020), Visual Capitalist (23 November 2020), www.visualcapitalist.com/50-years-gaming-history-revenue-stream, accessed 17 November 2023

35   Forbes, Markus Persson profile, *Forbes* (2023), www.forbes.com/profile/markus-persson, accessed 30 June 2023

36   C Gao, *Tencent's Wholly-Owned Subsidiary Miniclip Acquires Subway Surfers Developer SYBO* (*Superpixel,* 2022), www.superpixel.com/article/105286/tencents-wholly-owned-subsidiary-miniclip-acquires-subway-surfers-developer-sybo, accessed 30 June 2023

37   N Statt, *The Maker of Grand Theft Auto Just Bought Zynga in the Biggest Game Deal in History,* Protocol (10 January 2022), www.protocol.com/bulletins/take-two-acquires-zynga, accessed 30 June 2023

38   Microsoft News Center, *Microsoft to Acquire Activision Blizzard to Bring Joy and Community of Gaming to Everyone, Across Every Device*, Microsoft (18 January 2022), https://news.microsoft.com/2022/01/18/microsoft-to-acquire-activision-blizzard-to-bring-the-joy-and-community-of-gaming-to-everyone-across-every-device, accessed 30 June 2023

39   J Gvora, *Google Glass: What happened to the futuristic smart glasses?*, Screenrant (30 April 2023), https://screenrant.com/google-glass-smart-glasses-what-happened-explained, accessed 30 June 2023

40   D Wood, 'The Green Games Guide', ukie (25 March 2021), https://ukie.org.uk/greengamesguide, accessed 31 July 2023

41 Dove Self Esteem Squad game, www.dove.com/uk/dove-self-esteem-project/self-esteem-squad.html#!, accessed 31 July 2023

42 C Luongo, 'Zenni eyes esports expansion with three partnerships', ESI (15 April 2020), https://esportsinsider.com/2020/04/zenni-esports-partnerships, accessed 31 July 2023

43 A Kemp, 'Heinz challenges gamers to confront soil degradation in Fortnite', *The Drum* (16 March 2023), www.thedrum.com/news/2023/03/16/heinz-challenges-gamers-confront-soil-degradation-fortnite, accessed 30 June 2023

44 Heinz, 'Achieving 100% sustainable ketchup by 2025' (no date), www.heinz.co.uk/sustainable-ketchup-tomatoes, accessed 30 June 2023

45 SYBO Games, 'SYBO Games joins Lady Gaga's Born This Way Foundation #BeKind21 Campaign', *GlobalNewswire* (3 September 2021), www.globenewswire.com/en/news-release/2021/09/03/2291570/0/en/SYBO-Games-Joins-Lady-Gaga-s-Born-This-Way-Foundation-BeKind21-Campaign.html, accessed 30 June 2021

46 L Maguire, 'Balenciaga launches on Fortnite: What it means for luxury', *Vogue Business* (20 September 2021), www.voguebusiness.com/technology/balenciaga-launches-on-fortnite-what-it-means-for-luxury, accessed 30 June 2023

47 News, 'Announcing the Gran Turismo x Dior Collaboration', Gran Turismo (30 July 2022), www.gran-turismo.com/gb/gt7/news/00_3239408.html, accessed 31 July 2023

48 Gucci, 'Welcome to Gucci Town' (no date), www.gucci.com/us/en/st/stories/inspirations-and-codes/article/gucci-town-on-roblox, accessed 31 July 2023

49 PlanetPlay, 'Nitro Nation: Car Racing Game' (no date), https://planetplay.com/store/games/64406a720e9c692e071eed19, accessed 31 July 2023

50 The G20 Peoples' Climate Vote 2021, UNDP (25 October 2021), www.undp.org/publications/g20-peoples-climate-vote-2021, accessed 1 July 2023

51 IPCC, *Climate Change 2022: Impacts, Adaptation and Vulnerability* (IPCC, 2022), www.ipcc.ch/report/ar6/wg2, accessed 7 July 2023

52 D Takahashi, 'Tapjoy says 50% of mobile gamers prefer free ad-based games', Venture Beat (10 March 2022), https://venturebeat.com/games/tapjoy-says-50-of-mobile-gamers-prefer-free-ad-based-games, accessed 31 July 2023

53 C Bamford-Beattie, 'The positive and negative effects of video games – A guide, *Kidslox* (4 January 2022), https://kidslox.com/guide-to/positive-and-negative-effects-of-video-games, accessed 1 July 2023

54 UCSF Neuroscape (2018), https://neuroscape.ucsf.edu/technology/#neuroracer, accessed 31 January 2019

55 CJ Ferguson, 'Alternative routes of Christopher J Ferguson' (2021), www.christopherjferguson.com/NMPEPP%20Policy%20Statement%20Review.pdf; CJ Ferguson et al, 'A longitudinal analysis of shooter games and their relationship with conduct disorder and cself-reported delinquency', *Science Direct* (2018), www.sciencedirect.com/science/article/abs/pii/S0160252717302698, accessed 1 July 2023

56 C Buckle, 'Coronavirus: The impact on consumers worldwide', *GWI* (27 March 2020), www.gwi.com/webinars/coronavirus-multi-market-insights, accessed 1 July 2023

57 Newsround, 'Lockdown: Has playing video games helped you stay in touch with your friends?', CBBC (15 February 2021), www.bbc.co.uk/newsround/56068020, accessed 31 July 2023

58 M Barr, A Copeland-Stewart, 'Playing video games during the COVID-19 pandemic and effects on players' well-being', *Sage Journals*, Volume 17, Issue 1 (6 May 2021), https://doi.org/10.1177/15554120211017036, accessed 1 July 2023

59 A Grant @AdamMGrant, 'Instead of telling kids not to play…' (27 October 2022), www.instagram.com/p/CkOt2jqP2zE/?utm_source=ig_embed&utm_campaign=loading, accessed 7 July 2023

60 K Anderton, 'The impact of gaming: A benefit to society', *Forbes* (25 June 2018), www.forbes.com/sites/kevinanderton/2018/06/25/the-impact-of-gaming-a-benefit-to-society-infographic/?sh=480653d5269d, accessed 27 July 2023

61 P4 Annual Report 2019, 'Playing For The Planet, How video games can deliver for people and the

environment', UN Environment/GRID-Arendal (2019), https://c6e437facc6f704b.azureedge.net/media/Playing4ThePlanet/Files/p4pannualreport2019.pdf, accessed 1 July 2023

62 WEF, *How Do We Tackle the Fastest Growing Waste Stream on the Planet?* (9 February 2018), www.weforum.org/agenda/2018/02/how-do-we-tackle-the-fastest-growing-waste-stream-on-the-planet, accessed 12 Feb 2019

63 Pace and WEF, *A New Circular Vision for Electronics Time for a Global Reboot* (January 2019), www3.weforum.org/docs/WEF_A_New_Circular_Vision_for_Electronics.pdf, accessed 12 Feb 2019

64 I Khan, 'PS5 vs Xbox Series X: With great power comes greater electric bills', tom's guide (14 January 2021), www.tomsguide.com/news/ps5-vs-xbox-series-x-with-great-power-comes-greater-electric-bills, accessed 31 July 2023

65 C Asher, 'Playing dangerously: The environmental impact of video gaming consoles', *Mongabay* (25 October 2022), https://news.mongabay.com/2022/10/playing-dangerously-the-environmental-impact-of-video-gaming-consoles, accessed 1 July 2023

66 C Fletcher, 'Sustainability and the video gaming industry,' *Earth Org* (14 December 2021), https://earth.org/sustainability-and-the-video-gaming-industry, accessed 1 July 2023

67 Project Drawdown, 'A Drawdown-aligned framework for the gaming industry' (no date), https://drawdown.org/publications/a-drawdown-aligned-framework-for-the-gaming-industry, accessed 1 July 2023

68 N Raford, 'How gaming can be a force for good' (TED2022), www.ted.com/talks/noah_raford_how_gaming_can_be_a_force_for_good?language=en, accessed 5 July 2023

69 J Desjardins, 'In the race for 50 million users there's one clear winner - and it might surprise you', *WEF* (26 June 2018), www.weforum.org/agenda/2018/06/how-long-does-it-take-to-hit-50-million-users, accessed 1 July 2023

70 Project Drawdown, 'The world's leading resource for climate solutions' (no date), https://drawdown.org, accessed 1 July 2023

71 UNDP, 'The Peoples' Climate Vote' (UNDP, 2021), www.undp.org/publications/peoples-climate-vote, accessed 3 July 2023

72 IPCC, *Climate Change 2022: Impacts, Adaptation and Vulnerability* (IPCC, 2022), www.ipcc.ch/report/ar6/wg2, accessed 7 July 2023

73 J McVernon; H Vally, 'Did an accidental "blood plague" in World of Warcraft help scientists model Covid better? The results are in', *The Conversation* (23 August 2022), https://theconversation.com/did-an-accidental-blood-plague-in-world-of-warcraft-help-scientists-model-covid-better-the-results-are-in-188219, accessed 1 July 2023

74 ICL, 'Covid-19 behaviour tracker, Tracking global behaviours during the Covid-19 pandemic (no date), www.imperial.ac.uk/global-health-innovation/what-we-do/our-response-to-covid-19/covid-19-behaviour-tracker, accessed 1 July 2023

75 D Takahashi, *WHO and game companies launch #PlayApartTogether to promote physical distancing* (VentureBeat, 28 March 2020), https://venturebeat.com/business/who-and-game-companies-launch-playaparttogether-to-promote-physical-distancing, accessed 7 July 2023

76 Science Projects, 'Foldit: Playing a Game While Solving Protein Structures', Science Buddies (no date), www.sciencebuddies.org/science-fair-projects/project-ideas/BioMed_p008/medical-biotechnology/foldit-playing-a-game-while-solving-protein-structures, accessed 31 July 2023

77 Cooper, S., Khatib, F., Treuille, A. et al, 'Predicting protein structures with a multiplayer online game', *Nature* 466, 756–760 (2010), https://doi.org/10.1038/nature09304

78 J Markoff, 'In a Video Game, Tackling the Complexities of Protein Folding', *The New York Times* (9 August 2010), www.nytimes.com/2010/08/10/science/10gamers.html, accessed 31 July 2023

79 D Glaser, 'How video games stave off dementia', *The Guardian* (28 August 2016), www.theguardian.com/lifeandstyle/2016/aug/28/a-neuroscientist-explains-how-video-games-stave-off-dementia, accessed 31 July 2023

80 GREAT, 'Project kick-off: Games realising effective and affective transformation', *EduTec* (2023), https://edutec.science/project-start-games-realising-effective-and-affective-transformation-great, accessed 1 July 2023

81   Stockholm Resilience Centre, 'Sustainable Development
     Goals' (28 February 2017), www.stockholmresilience.org/
     research/research-news/2017-02-28-contributions-to-
     agenda-2030.html, accessed 10 October 2023

82   UN Environment Programme, *Playing for the Planet
     Alliance's Annual Impact Report*, UNEP (9 March 2023),
     www.unep.org/resources/report/playing-planet-alliances-
     2022-annual-impact-report, accessed 5 July 2023

83   D Mensah-Bonsu et al, 'Green Game Jam Player Survey
     2022', Playing for the Planet Alliance (2022), https://www.
     playing4theplanet.org/post/ggj22-survey, accessed 31 July
     2023

84   D Mensah-Bonsu et al, 'Green Game Jam Player Survey
     2022', Playing for the Planet Alliance (2022), https://
     www.playing4theplanet.org/post/ggj22-survey, accessed
     31 July 2023

85   T Gerken, 'Ukraine war: Fortnite owner Epic Games raises
     £37m for humanitarian efforts, BBC News (24 March 2022),
     www.bbc.co.uk/news/technology-60850729, accessed
     31 July 2023

86   R Valentine, 'Riot Games' Social Impact Fund has raised
     $10m so far', *Games Industry.biz* (12 May 2020), https://
     www.gamesindustry.biz/riot-games-donates-usd10k-each-
     to-30-non-profit-organisations, accessed 1 July 2023

87   Vericast, 'Consumer Intel Report, The cautious return to
     a new world' (2021), https://insight-hs.vericast.com/
     hubfs/2021/2021-Consumer-Intel-Report-2022-11-CS1261.
     pdf, accessed 1 July 2023

88   Charities Aid Foundation, Giving Through Gaming
     (2017), www.cafonline.org/docs/default-source/about-
     us-publications/gamingsurveyinfographic_040117.
     pdf?sfvrsn=0, accessed 12 February 2019

89   M Barr, A Copeland-Stewart, 'Playing video games during
     the COVID-19 pandemic and effects on players' well-
     being', *Sage Journals*, Volume 17, Issue 1 (2021), https://doi.
     org/10.1177/15554120211017036, accessed 1 July 2023

90   Sustainability at Unity, 2022 ESG Report, https://unity.
     com/esg-environment, accessed 7 July 2023

91   Project Drawdown, 'A Drawdown-aligned framework for
     the gaming industry, (no date), https://drawdown.org/
     publications/a-drawdown-aligned-framework-for-the-
     gaming-industry, accessed 1 July 2023

92   Making Wildlife Part Of Everyday Life, Internet of Elephants (no date), www.internetofelephants.com, accessed 1 July 2023

93   Liftoff, *Mobile Gaming Apps Report: 2019 user acquisition trends and benchmarks* (Liftoff, 2019), https://liftoff.io/wp-content/uploads/2019/08/Liftoff_2019_Mobile_Gaming_Apps_Report.pdf, accessed 5 July 2023

94   Project Drawdown, 'A Drawdown-aligned framework for the gaming industry' (March 2023), https://drawdown.org/publications/a-drawdown-aligned-framework-for-the-gaming-industry, accessed 1 July 2023

95   Project Drawdown: Job Function Action Guides (no date), https://drawdown.org/programs/drawdown-labs/job-function-action-guides, accessed 1 July 2023

96   Project Drawdown, 'A Drawdown-aligned framework for the gaming industry' (March 2023), https://drawdown.org/publications/a-drawdown-aligned-framework-for-the-gaming-industry, accessed 1 July 2023

97   Geena Davis Institute (2023), https://seejane.org, accessed 1 July 2023

98   Riot Games, 'The Underrepresented Founders Program' (22 September 2020), www.riotgames.com/en/news/the-underrepresented-founders-program, accessed 31 July 2023

99   L Rees, 'ustwo's Jennifer Estaris on gaming's potential for positive change', *Pocket Gamer* (27 January 2023), www.pocketgamer.biz, accessed 6 July 2023

100 D Robson, '"The 3.5% rule": How a small minority can change the world', BBC Future (14 May 2019), www.bbc.com/future/article/20190513-it-only-takes-35-of-people-to-change-the-world, accessed 27 July 2023

101 J Yap, 'Charity 2.0 puts users as force behind social change', *ZDNet* (14 January 2011), www.zdnet.com/article/charity-2-0-puts-users-as-force-behind-social-change, accessed 30 December 2018

102 Y Solheim, 'Making strides for a more sustainable future', Niantic (3 May 2019), https://nianticlabs.com/news/earthday2019recap, accessed 10 August 2023

103 Call of Duty Endowment: Let's get veterans back to work (no date), www.callofdutyendowment.org, accessed 27 July 2023

104 Little Chicken, 'Safari Central Starts Kickstarter Campaign' (no date), www.littlechicken.nl/safari-central, accessed 31 July 2023

105   The Cybersmile Foundation, 'High School Story
      Partnership Ends' (no date), www.cybersmile.org/news/
      high-school-story-partnership-comes-to-an-end, accessed
      31 July 2023

106   UN-Habitat, 'The Block by Block Playbook: Using
      Minecraft as a participatory design tool in urban design
      and governance' (2021), https://unhabitat.org/the-block-
      by-block-playbook-using-minecraft-as-a-participatory-
      design-tool-in-urban-design-and, accessed 31 July 2023

107   Reason Digital, 'How video games are being used for
      social good' (3 October 2013), https://reasondigital.
      com/blog/using-video-games-for-social-good, accessed
      30 December 2018

108   L Gordon, 'Can video games change people's minds about
      the climate crisis?' *The Guardian* (26 January 2023), www.
      theguardian.com, accessed 6 July 2023

109   Ubisoft, 2021–22 Universal Registration Document and
      Annual Financial Report (2022), https://downloads.
      ctfassets.net/8aefmxkxpxwl/44Uv9g0KnmBI5KlAgh
      iJh/cdb36cc23a9930832acd8ecbb4dcbe61/UBISOFT_
      DEU_21-22_MEL_INTERACTIF_UK_160622.pdf, accessed
      1 July 2023

110   L Gordon, 'Can video games change people's minds about
      the climate crisis?' *The Guardian* (26 January 2023), www.
      theguardian.com, accessed 6 July 2023

111   After Climate, www.afterclimate.com.au/about, accessed
      31 July 2023

112   N Dornieden, 'Nintendo Switch is the most eco-friendly
      console of this generation' (23 February 2021), www.
      imore.com/nintendo-switch-most-eco-friendly-console-
      generation, accessed 27 July 2023

113   B Smith, 'Microsoft will be carbon negative by 2030',
      Microsoft blog (16 January 2020), https://blogs.microsoft.
      com/blog/2020/01/16/microsoft-will-be-carbon-negative-
      by-2030, accessed 27 July 2023

114   C Liu, 'New Microsoft toolkit will measure real-time Xbox
      energy use', *Bloomberg UK* (2023), www.bloomberg.com/
      news/articles/2023-03-22/new-microsoft-toolkit-will-
      measure-real-time-xbox-energy-use, accessed 1 July 2023

115   Rovio, 'Taking environmental action – playing for the
      planet and beyond' (22 October 2020), www.rovio.com/
      articles/taking-environmental-action-playing-for-the-
      planet-and-beyond, accessed 27 July 2023

116 I Paananen, 'My take on Supercell in 2019 as we enter our second decade', *Supercell* (2020), https://supercell.com/en/news/my-take-supercell-2019-we-enter-our-second-decade/7427, accessed 27 July 2023

117 UKIE, 'Helping games business to take action against climate change', *Green Games Guide* (2021), https://ukie.org.uk/sustainability, accessed 1 July 2023

118 Suomen Pelinkehittäjät, Neogames, 'CO_2 emission calculation model' (2022), https://neogames.fi/wp-content/uploads/2022/03/CO2-emission-calculation-model-Finland.pdf, accessed 1 July 2023

119 C Whittle et al, *The Environmental Game Design Playbook* (IGDA, 2022), https://igda-website.s3.us-east-2.amazonaws.com/wp-content/uploads/2022/04/06100719/EnvironmentalGameDesignPlaybook_Alpha_Release_Adj.pdf, accessed 1 July 2023

120 The Fair Play Alliance: About page, https://fairplayalliance.org/about, accessed 1 July 2023

121 D Takahashi, *WHO and game companies launch #PlayApartTogether to promote physical distancing* (VentureBeat, 28 March 2020), www.venturebeat.com, accessed 7 July 2023

122 Games Aid, www.gamesaid.org, accessed 27 July 2023

123 Humble Bundle, www.humblebundle.com, accessed 27 July 2023

Resources

To learn more about the industry efforts to fight climate change, and the Playing for the Planet Alliance, visit www.playing4theplanet.org. The Green Game Jam is part of this – find out more at www.playing4theplanet.org/green-game-jam-2023.

In the book, we discussed the game-changing work of Playmob, which used games in over fifty countries to change climate policy and increase their NDCs to help achieve the goals set out in the Paris Climate Change Agreement. You can read the report, which was an output of this work, here: www.undp.org/publications/peoples-climate-vote. This data was also used at the G20 – www.undp.org/publications/g20-peoples-climate-vote-2021 – and in the 2022 IPCC report, which can be read here: www.ipcc.ch/report/sixth-assessment-report-working-group-ii.

We discussed the importance of platforms in this space of games for good and how new players in the market such as PlanetPlay can be hugely important to unlock the power of good from our play time. Find out more about this platform at www.planetplay.com.

For further resources on how to implement sustainability into a games studio, these extremely useful examples could also inspire other sectors:

- Project Drawdown: https://drawdown.org/publications/a-drawdown-aligned-framework-for-the-gaming-industry

- IGDA: https://igda-website.s3.us-east-2.amazonaws.com/wp-content/uploads/2022/04/06100719/EnvironmentalGameDesignPlaybook_Alpha_Release_Adj.pdf

- NeoGames: https://neogames.fi/wp-content/uploads/2022/03/CO2-emission-calculation-model-Finland.pdf

- UKIE: https://ukie.org.uk/sustainability

- SpaceApe's Carbon Neutrality blog plus useful links: https://spaceapegames.com/green

To read more on initiatives set up by games companies and be inspired by the art of the possible:

- The *Call of Duty* Endowment raises funds for war veterans. The Endowment's impact report is one of the most succinct we have seen in terms of impact delivered and how this affects the US economy. Read more at www. callofdutyendowment.org

- Ubisoft has made tremendous efforts to link sustainability to business activity and even executive remuneration. Read more in its Annual Report: https://downloads.ctfassets.net /8aefmxkxpxwl/44Uv9g0KnmBI5KlAghiJh/ cdb36cc23a9930832acd8ecbb4dcbe61/UBISOFT_ DEU_21-22_MEL_INTERACTIF_UK_160622.pdf

- The EA Positive Play Charter outlines how players should behave and rules to protect players in EA games – www.ea.com/ commitments/positive-play/charter

About PlanetPlay

Every book makes an impact – with thanks to PlanetPlay

This book is intended to have a positive impact on people and the planet, and with every book sold, funds will be donated to climate positive projects through PlanetPlay, a not-for-profit platform dedicated to enabling gamers to support the planet while they play.

To unlock your impact from this book, scan the QR code and follow the instructions online.

Scan me

PlanetPlay was created to help the games industry and its playing community easily and accessibly contribute to climate positive action.

With its passionate 3.1 billion player following, the games industry has enormous potential to support and influence climate positive change globally. Games are a unique platform through which to inspire, educate and mobilise players in support of the climate and ancillary causes.

PlanetPlay has created the world's first climate-conscious marketplace, where players can buy games, in-game items and real-life items all in support of the planet. This, combined with collaborating on uniquely engaging in-game events, PlanetPlay are raising funds and awareness for the fight against climate change.

PlanetPlay is a Sphaira Innovation brand. Sphaira Innovation is a not-for-profit entity dedicated to reversing the climate crisis through the power of people and technology.

Acknowledgements

Wwe want to say a huge thank you to those who have made this book the best it could be. Thank you to Steffen Lyhne, Rasmus Møller, Adam Collier and Trym Johansen for the fun visuals and magical illustrations sprinkled throughout as treats for our readers' eyes, and of course for the front cover which we hope will be seen and enjoyed by millions globally. You have made this important book sparkle even more.

Thank you to Susanne Sayers, Nicolas Hunsinger, Olga Ostrowska and Alan Gershenfeld for spending your time reading, reviewing and providing valuable feedback to make this book punchy and more appealing to our readers. Thank you to Lottie Dean who worked tirelessly to provide the most up-to-date industry statistics and check the data was accurate as of 2022/23.

Thank you to those sticking their necks out to make the games industry a positive force for good. So many people to mention, but for starters, big shouts out to Sam Barratt, Trista Patterson, Deborah Mensah-Bonsu, Lisa Pak, Siiri Maekekae, Phil Spencer, Jim Ryan, Kieren Mayers, Asi Burak, Rhea Loucas, Paula Angela Escuadra, John Hanke, Ilkka Paananen, Alan Gershenfeld, Hunter Bulkeley, Noah Falstein, Dr Ben Abraham, Susanna Pollack, Ian Livingstone, Rob Small, Robert Antokol, Tamzin Taylor, Marc Merrill, Matt Fischer, Marina Psaros, Nicolas Hunsinger, Arnauld Fayolle, Iris Gardet-Hadengue, Yennie Solheim Fuller, Jennifer Estaris, Murari Vasudevan, Olga Ostrowska, Paul Flanagan, Heini Kaihu, Joost Schuur, Lou Fawcett, Gareth Jones, Tommi Lappalainen, Jose Saarniniemi, Nic Walker and Joost Vervoort. To all those we have not mentioned, we know you are out there.

We could not have written this book without the support of the teams of those we interviewed. These amazing humans were extremely responsive and diligent in making sure we carried out our interviews, and that all the quotes and mentions of the interviewees are accurate and have been approved. They were key to us having some of the most important voices in the games industry represented in our book. Huge thank you to:

- Sophie Orlando (Xbox)

- Brian Cairns (Riot)

- Viivi Ali-Löytty (Supercell)

- Kelly Budde (Miniclip)

- Debbie Lloyd (Alfred London)

- Danielle Segal (Playtika)

- Jonny Thaw (Niantic)

- Rachel Davies (EA)

- Jo Bartlett (EA)

- Peter Nguyen (Apple)

- Philip Hickey (Sybo)

To the games industry and those sticking their necks out to make it a positive force for good. Keep doing what you do, and we will steer this ship in the right direction.

The Authors

Jude Ower

Jude Ower has been championing games for good for over twenty years, starting off in the games for education space and moving into turning entertainment games into a force for good. She is the Founder and CEO of Playmob, a market insights platform gathering public sentiment through games. Playmob has enabled the UN to collect the world's largest data set on climate attitudes – data that is being used in fifty-two countries for climate policy decisions, and has also been used for the G20 and the IPCC Report in 2022.

Learn more about Jude's work:

⊕ www.playmob.com

Mathias Nørvig

Mathias Nørvig has been fighting for a better planet since he joined the student council at Holbæk lille Skole in the late nineties. He volunteered in NGOs while learning the ins and outs of the corporate world, and the institutional investment experience he gained in Sub-Saharan Africa combined with his stint at PwC gave him a different toolbox to a traditional gaming CEO. At SYBO, he manages the most downloaded game of all time, *Subway Surfers*, making sure that it portrays diversity, inclusivity and as much sustainability as possible in a way that inspires millions of players to care while enjoying playful moments.

Both Jude and Mathias are also Co-founders of the Playing for the Planet Alliance, which launched at the UN General Assembly in September 2019. The Alliance is a group of fifty+ forward-thinking games studios and publishers, such as Supercell, Rovio, Ubisoft, SYBO, Niantic, Xbox and PlayStation, with a collective reach of 1.4 billion monthly players.

Learn more about Mathias' work:

🌐 www.sybogames. com